WHERE IS GOD WHEN BAD THINGS HAPPEN?

6832 Convent Blvd.
Sylvania, OH 43560

WHERE IS GOD WHEN BAD THINGS HAPPEN?

Horace O. Duke

Cover Design:
Scott Wannemuehler

Library of Congress Catalog Number
91-75428

ISBN 0-87029-239-0

Published by Abbey Press
St. Meinrad Archabbey
St. Meinrad, Indiana 47577

Dedicated with love

to a gracious woman—

my wife, Nancy

Contents

Acknowledgments

I offer profound thanks to those who have supported me in my efforts to write this book. They include friends and colleagues at GTF: Sr. Joan A. Murray, OP, of Westmont, Illinois, Rev. Douglas Lind of Westport, Connecticut, Rev. Jerry F. Angevine of Greenville, North Carolina, Fr. Frank Farrante, CMF, of San Gabriel, California, and Rev. Ted Harris of Memphis, Tennessee. Also, Dr. Wayne G. Rollins, Assumption College, Worcester, Massachusetts, Dr. John H. Morgan, Graduate Theological Fellowship, Notre Dame, Indiana, and Dr. James Ashbrook, who read my manuscript and encouraged me in this undertaking. I will never forget their generosity of time and advice. A special word of thanks to my friend and mentor, Mrs. Betty Heald-Williams, R.S.W., for her personal encouragement, professional challenge, and many hours of reading. Thanks also to Mrs. Jeanette Lortz for her editing. Finally, sincere thanks to my colleagues in pastoral care at Providence Medical Center, Portland, Oregon, and the chaplain interns of 1987 to 1989 in the clinical pastoral education program for their encouragement and perceptive critiques.

Chaplain Pete Zagel. Born December 14, 1926.

Diagnosed with amyotrophic lateral sclerosis on June 17, 1985. Died January 19, 1987, from complications of ALS.

Chaplain Horace O. Duke. Born May 15, 1935.

Diagnosed with amyotrophic lateral sclerosis on July 12, 1985. Medical judgment pronounced Horace Duke free of ALS in November 1987.

This book is in honor of Pete Zagel and his "kin."

Introduction

This book is one of inspirational theology based on the lives of people whose names are not Moses, Isaiah, or St. Paul. Their real names are not in this book and many of the details about them are altered intentionally to assure their anonymity. They are not great people who have done extraordinary things. They are ordinary people, the kind you rarely notice as you pass them on the street. You stand next to them in an elevator or checkout line in the supermarket. They are people who, perhaps like you or someone you know, have suffered grievously. They have been hurt in life and they wonder why.

This book deals with two simple questions: *Where* is God when bad things happen? and *how* can an understanding of *where* God is make any difference in a person's life?

This book is about God but is not a defense of God. It is an effort to face some of the harsh realities of human experience and to discover what these realities teach us about God. It doesn't evade hard questions nor manipulate answers to fit nicely into a pretty package. It is a look at tragic[1] and evil[2] events apart from easy notions and centuries of well-defended religious thinking. It is a practical look at the way God is involved in the kind of life you and I live every day in a world of messy kitchens, houses that need painting, and oversized corporate boardrooms.

I share in these pages the tragedies and suffering of fellow human beings, what I have learned about God as I faced the death of family members, the good and bad in my personal life, the period of time when I lived with the diagnosis of ALS (amyotrophic lateral sclerosis, commonly known as Lou Gehrig's disease) and the prognosis of

1

having only two more years to live.

As you follow the pattern of this book, you will find several dominant threads that hold it together. These are the stories of some very special people who were introduced to pain and suffering early in life. They were all raped before they reached their tenth birthday. First is Thomas. He provides the central thread. My encounter with Thomas and his blunt question compelled me to write this book.

Thomas and I met only briefly when he was a patient in the hospital where I have served as chaplain for more than seventeen years. This book emerges out of one single hour in our lives—an hour that radically changed my thinking about God and in many ways changed my life. As I struggled with Thomas's questions about life and God, I had an experience that mirrored that of the patriarch Jacob (Gn 32:22-32).[3] In my experience with Thomas I wrestled with myself and with what I understand to be Holy. Like Jacob who wrestled with God and himself, I came away with a blessing that challenges me to "walk differently."

Thomas's simple question about God and evil is a theme common to each of the people you will meet. Thomas was sexually abused as a child. As a young man, one question haunted him: "Where was God when I was raped?" Thomas is a real individual. His story is true. But Thomas's story is so poignant because he is a living composite of multitudes of nameless boys and girls, men and women, a living compilation of all who have experienced rape and are left to deal with the inescapable conundrum: If God is good, if God is all-powerful, if this world is in the hands of God, *where* is God and *what* is God doing when we are innocent victims of merciless evil or random tragedy?

In his book, *When Bad Things Happen to Good People* (New York: Schocken Books, 1981), Rabbi Harold S. Kushner provides helpful insights for dealing with the common "why" kind of questions. Why do evil acts occur? Why are there random tragedies in the world? Why do I suffer without just cause? Kushner concludes that God does not send the bad things to us. God does not cause evil things to happen, nor does God actually allow the bad to occur. Kushner offers a philosophical-theological answer to these questions based on the Hebrew scriptures: That is just the way life is. The rain falls and the sun shines on the good and the bad; both get sunburned or soaking wet when they are unprotected. Kushner's belief that God is not out to get us is assuring. His understanding that God is available to help us face life is comforting.

Philip Yancey has also tried to make sense out of what appears to be the seemly side of God's relation to men and women. Though he states it with a clearly Christian world view, Yancey comes to much the same conclusion as Kushner. In his candid work, *Disappointment with God* (Grand Rapids, Michigan: Zondervan, 1988), Yancey goes so far as to postulate some of the possible reasons why God is silent and unresponsive in the face of our cries for help and our pleadings for answers to our questions. For Kushner, God has nothing to do with the evil and tragic events that occur. For Yancey, the questions like the one Thomas raised are valid and should not be branded as sacrilegious. However, Yancey sees in the final word that God is still a God who is in control of the affairs of humankind. Thus, Yancey's God allows evil and may, at times, use what appears on a human or "lower" level to be evil. Yancey suggests that God allows or uses evil for a higher—and unknown to us—divine purpose. Yancey's conclusion is that nearly everyone faces disappointments in life. Our task, then, is to choose to face the disappointments of tragic and evil events with God or without God. Yancey's disappointments do not focus on God, but rather on one's lack of faith. It appears to be a faith that calls for the traditional belief that no matter what happens God is in control.

Thomas asked: *"Where was God when I was raped? Where was he?"*

The second person you meet is Sarah. Thomas made me face the question, but Sarah pressed me to consider a new kind of answer. Sarah is a person I call a genuine theologian-in-residence-of-everyday-life. Sarah spent her childhood and early teen years in an orphanage in Canada. She was taken from her small native North American village when her father went to prison. He confessed to a crime Sarah is still convinced he did not commit. A staff member in the orphanage sexually abused Sarah. She was raped routinely with the small smooth curved end of a fire iron. At those times, she remembers clearly the crucifix that hung on the wall of the little room. Sarah prayed for God to help her. Each week God watched and each week God did nothing but hang on the cross. Sarah knew about the God who suffered, but even more important was her discovery about the intent of God's suffering and what it could mean to her.

Karen provides the third major thread in a tapestry of theology-from-everyday-life. Karen—like Sarah, Thomas, and several others you will meet—was also an innocent victim of rape when she was a child. Her story is the most tragic and difficult to understand. Karen was raised in a home where several family members used her for their sexual gratification. Karen lets you share in her search for spiritual and psychological freedom from the consequences of her childhood experiences. Karen challenged me the most. She allowed me to accompany her on a daring journey into fear, doubt, and faith. In the realities of her therapy I encountered the meaning of my belief in a God who is immersed in human experience. Karen dared to examine the despair of Thomas and the hope of Sarah and to test them in her own life. But you shall see that it is as much my struggle for a meaningful belief about God and evil as that of Karen's. In fact, Karen and the others are the arena where I have worked out some of my own long-hidden encounters with doubt and faith. These special people compelled me to face my doubts and my faith. They inspired me to be open and honest about my doubts and my faith. They have helped me come to a new kind of peace and resolve about both of them.

Thomas, Sarah, Karen, and the others have richly blessed my life. Together they taught me an understanding of God that I did not learn in the seminary. They helped me gain a new understanding of *where* God is the moment bad things happen to us. To have confidence in a relationship with God, one needs to know where God is during dark and devastating moments. It is one thing to believe God does not send bad things to us. But it is something else to know *where* God is and precisely *what* God is doing when they do come to us.

Thomas, Sarah, and Karen did not attend a theological seminary. But they tried to answer some of the questions a seminary education is all about. I call them theologians-in-residence-of-everyday-life. They would insist they know little about theology. But theology is simply a way of thinking and talking about God. It is an effort to make sense out of who God is in relationship to us. Thomas, Sarah, and Karen are theologians in the biblical tradition. They have a practical theology that comes out of their life experiences.

What they taught me has changed the way I look at myself, the world, and most important, the way I view God. Learning from them has helped me better understand myself and how to handle difficulties in my life. It has helped me understand *how* God is actually involved with me in the hard times. Perhaps what I have learned from them will help you or someone you know. That is the primary purpose of this book.

I offer a caution. This book is not for everyone. Some people may find it too blunt, filled with too many questions and not enough answers. Worse yet, the answers may be too demanding. Some may feel it is irreverent, that it questions things that believers should never have doubts about. At times, it is easier to live with unexplored questions than to face the kind of faith called for in such a risky endeavor. This is a book about faith. However, it is the kind of faith that stands against all odds and hangs in there when the whirlwinds of life and death wreak havoc. It is the faith of people who country-western singer Willie Nelson sings are "bent over from running against the wind."

This book is based on a graduate project designed to meet the requirement for the doctorate of ministry degree in pastoral counseling with the Graduate Theological Foundation, Notre Dame, Indiana. My colleague consultants in the Foundation asked me bluntly, "Why are you writing this book?" My response was:

"I want people to know that there is at least one minister who has the guts to raise the questions that they have in their minds and hearts—that it is OK to talk out loud about some of the thoughts that are in the shadows of our hearts as we recite our creeds and statements of faith on Saturday and Sunday morning. I want people to know they are not alone in their fearful and hard questions, that they are not bad, or disloyal, or lacking in faith when they have doubts and are perplexed over the inconsistencies of good and evil they see in life. People need to know that God is not upset with us when we grapple with the teachings of our churches. God is more upset when we allow the traditions of our institutions and cultural norms to become so revered that we can no longer separate them from the original events that they represent and about which they teach."

There is a real sense in which our worst fears are true. We are in this world on our own; no one is going to live for us. If we make it, it is because we dare to do it. These are things I have learned from victims of evil. They have taught me how much God loves us and is intimately involved in our lives. There is a God, and that God is with us! But the *way* God is with us and involved in our lives may be different from our own conceptions.

Stories abound about people who were *almost* murdered or raped, or *almost* killed in a tragic accident, but whom an unexpected turn of events miraculously saved. These stories are often testimonies of praise and gratitude. They are told as examples of what happens if "you just trust God" or "really have faith." This book is not about people with those kinds of stories. Those stories may be true but they are only a small fraction of the stories of people confronted with the tragic and evil parts of life. This book is about the vast number of people who have a different testimony.

Some readers may disagree. Nevertheless, the testimonies of Thomas and his kin demand a deep kind of faith and trust in life and in God. It is one thing to believe and be grateful when you have escaped a maniac's butcher knife or a rapist's degrading painful assault. But what do you do when you feel the pain, see the blood—and it is yours! How do you go on believing and trusting when those memories continue to haunt you? How do you trust and believe in people when others do those kinds of things to you? How do you trust a God who protects others but lets evil and bad things happen to you?

This book is told in narrative style about real people and true things. It may read at times like a short story, at other times like a novel. The reader may occasionally find my indirect manner confusing, but I believe it is worth your consideration. I have something to tell you, but I am more interested in what you tell yourself as you read my words. May you discover something new and meaningful for yourself in the process.

I am dealing with the greatest of all mysteries—the mystery of God and how God relates to individual human experience. It is a mystery I cannot solve, and I have come to the conclusion that there is not a one-and-only final answer to this mystery. In fact, the moment we think we know the fullness of God and the secrets to predicting what God can and will do in any and all given situations, we have succumbed to the greatest of all human follies. In that moment, we make ourselves God. In that moment, we enact Eden and eat again of the forbidden fruit and have lost all hope of paradise.

If you expect to find the answer to the question of good and evil in these pages, you will be disappointed. But if you dare to consider a different point of view in your approach to life, to faith, to God, you just may find....

NOTES

1. *Tragedy* denotes an event of destruction, death, or grave emotional

and/or physical suffering that occurs as the result of anything that is void of human evil intent. A tornado, a natural phenomenon, occurs as the result of a combination of natural forces and conditions. When a tornado occurs in a farming town in Texas, it is a tragedy—thirty people die, 121 are injured. But it is not an act of evil resulting from intentional or unintentional human will.

It is more than tragic when a person driving under the influence of alcohol or drugs kills a family. Their death is the result of action that is evil in its disregard for the life and well-being of others.

2. *Evil* in this book refers to the concept that M. Scott Peck notes in *The People of the Lie:* "...that force...that seeks to kill life or liveliness...goodness is its opposite." In the words of Peck's eight-year-old son, "Why, Daddy, evil is 'live' spelled backward" (New York: Simon & Schuster, Inc., 1983, pp. 42-43). Evil is in opposition to life; it is anything which opposes life forces, described throughout the Bible as violation of good. It is opposite to Jesus' stated purpose in his life: "I have come that they may have life and have it abundantly" (Jn 10:10). Evil in this context relates to tragic events caused by the willful actions of human beings, taken with the intent to kill, or destroy, or harm. The tornado in Saragosa, Texas, on May 23, 1987, was a tragedy. Auschwitz was an act of evil.

3. Jacob wrestles with a man during the night. Just who this strange man was is not clear. He has been interpreted as an angel, or God, or Jacob's deepest self. Jacob struggled with him as if his life were at stake. The result was that Jacob received a blessing which changed his life. Because of Jacob's discovery about himself and God that night, his name was changed from Jacob, "supplanter or deceiver," to Israel, "one who rules with God." Jacob's life was also radically changed as the result of his discovery.

CHAPTER ONE

THE QUESTION: "Where Was God When I Was Raped?"

"I'll start, Chaplain," Thomas blurted.

He was twenty-four years old. There was still a boyish cast to his face, but something in his eyes denied innocence. His eyes spoke of dark alleys and long nights.

"Where was God when I was raped?"

Thomas's question was blunt and unexpected. His words dismissed the silence that often prevails during the first minutes of a spiritual values therapy group. I have learned to be comfortable with this silence. It speaks only of an awkwardness that patients feel when they talk about their problems and what they believe—or do not believe—about life, themselves, and God.

A mental health program holistic in approach must consider a person's religious beliefs in developing a treatment plan. People are often under a delusion about life, and their religious beliefs become a part of their delusion. But religious beliefs are not delusions. Human beings live by their beliefs—regardless of what those beliefs are based upon or the disposition of that belief toward good or ill. Human behavior is deeply rooted in a system of beliefs.

Spiritual values groups on a mental health ward provide a setting where people can talk about their beliefs and discover ways to make optimum use of them to deal constructively with their mental health needs. I have led many such groups during my seventeen years as a hospital chaplain. My experience continues to make one thing certain; namely, that one's religious, irreligious, or nonreligious beliefs are enmeshed in the strength and weakness of one's mental health. Competent therapy cannot effectively address one separate from the other.

> *"Where was he?"* Thomas continued. *"I was just a kid! I needed help. How could he let things like that happen? Where was he when I was being abused—raped again and again! Where in the hell was he? What was he doing?"*

Feet shuffled, eyes turned up and down, throats cleared. Thomas's voice cracked with anger and agony. Many who find themselves caught between the reality of pain and despair and the elusive dream of relief and hope ask the same question.

"That's a tough question. But it is real," I said aloud to the group. The words "tough" and "real" echoed in my head, and from within a critical voice taunted, *"Sometimes you are so profound."*

My pastoral ministry with hospital patients has forced me to deal with hard questions. Psychiatric patients have a way of raising them routinely. I had faced Thomas's question before, yet this time it was different. I am still not sure what made it different. Perhaps it was because Thomas was a male. Perhaps it was Thomas; perhaps it was me. I do know I had never felt so helpless and at a loss for words. Perhaps the helplessness was the difference. I didn't suppress it, allowing myself to feel the helplessness. It was too important and too real to deny.

Professionals find it hard to allow themselves to feel helpless. We have the illusion that we must always be in control. We devise endless means to avoid our vulnerabilities. Perhaps that is why we get stale and stop growing, and co-workers find us professional but unreal. Helplessness often forces us to re-examine, to rethink, and to dare look at things in a new light.

I struggled to give an intelligent response to Thomas. As the minutes dragged on, sweat began to trickle down the middle of my back. The implications of this kind of question had troubled me throughout my thirty-five years of ministry. I had grown up believing in a God who is good, who is all-powerful. My God had the whole world in his hands. Where is the good and all-powerful God who has the world in hand when little boys and girls are raped? I had never resolved that question. Over the years I discovered that questions such as this were best forgotten when possible. Overscheduling, hard work at being successful, and good intentions sometimes help one forget.

Thomas's question goes beyond why bad things happen to good people. The existence of evil and tragic happenings are well-documented parts of human experience. From the beginning of time, philosophers and theologians have pondered the mystery of evil. Why does it exist? Where did it come from? These are valid questions with a variety of answers. However, Thomas's question pushed them aside. His concern was personal, more urgent, and practical.

Thomas was not trying to understand the existence of evil nor was he questioning the existence of God. As a child, Thomas was taught to believe in God—a God who is good, a God who is loving and takes care of little boys. Where was this good and loving God who takes care of little boys *while he was being raped?*

Thomas's question is also universal: "Where is God when evil prevails over good? What is God doing? How is God involved when bad things happen to people?" The English psychoanalyst Ernest Jones makes an interesting observation about the theological concept of Divine Providence: "What one really wishes to know about the Divine Purpose," he notes, "is its intention *toward oneself.*"[1] Jones also moves beyond the existence of good and evil to the more practical issue: What can one assume about the intention of a Divine Providence in any given situation? Paul W. Pruyser, a Presbyterian layman and noted clinical psychologist with the Menninger Foundation, addressed the same idea in his book, *The Minister as Diagnostician.* Pruyser writes: "Abstract doctrinal definitions of Providence are one thing——coming to terms with its personal import is quite another." He adds, "Troubled persons are understandably upset about the ratio of goodwill and ill will that comes their way."[2]

Can I know what to expect from God when I face bad things? I have lived most of my life with a kind of smug assurance that God is on my side. When I was sick or in trouble I always assured myself that somehow God would take care of me. But I had never been sexually assaulted or abused. To be honest, when I sat with people like Thomas I squirmed a bit at my smug assurance of being somewhat elite.

The writers of the Hebrew scriptures give evidence of this same kind of special relationship to God that insured safety. They often called attention to God's good intention toward Israel and through Israel to the world. God's good intention toward people is a central theme in the New Testament. The Gospel writers presented the angelic announcement of the birth of Jesus as an example of this claim: God's intention is "peace on earth." God's "goodwill" is toward the inhabitants of the earth (Lk 2:14). Is this a general intention toward

11

nations and groups or is this good intention extended to individuals?

The central thesis of most Christian theology is that God's intention is good toward every human being. The heart of the biblical message is that God loves the world! God can be trusted. God's intention toward people is good (Jn 3:16).

If God's intention toward little boys is good, where was that good intention when Thomas was raped? What was God doing? This kind of question is not uncommon in the Bible. Notice David's words in Psalm 35:

> ...Lord, fight those fighting me...For though I did them no wrong, yet
> they laid a trap for me...These evil men swear to a lie...They accuse
> me of things I have never even heard about...I am sinking down into
> death. Lord, how long will you stand there doing nothing?[3]

David claims to be innocent of any wrong that would merit the situation he was facing. David implies that he could accept all that was happening if it were the result of his own misconduct. But to suffer because of the sheer evil of others was unbearable. Why? Because David believed God's intention toward him was good. David understood that God should be there to bail him out when evil besieged him. Tyndale's *Living Study Bible* catches the pathos in David's situation: "Lord how long will you stand there doing nothing?" There's the rub—standing there and doing nothing. David was confident that God knew he had done nothing wrong. But just in case God had forgotten, David refreshed God's memory. David's expectation was simple. He expected God to intervene in his behalf. David knew people were not always dependable. But God?

David's problem was real, much like the dilemmas many of us face from time to time. His belief and his experience did not match up.

David's question merges with that of Thomas. They join a chorus of millions of abused and wronged people from every generation who have called out for rescue from the onslaught of evil and random tragedies, only to have their words fade into the silence of an unresponsive universe. In moments such as these, I have been troubled by thoughts such as those often attributed to the eighteenth century German philosopher, Martin Heidegger: "I do not deny the existence of God, I simply call attention to his absence."

C. S. Lewis, the noted Cambridge and Oxford professor, is remembered as one of the great intellectual men of Christian faith in the twentieth century. One biographer called Lewis the "apostle to the skeptics." A confirmed bachelor, at the age of 58 he married Joy Davidman, an American poet with two children. After four brief and happy years of marriage, Joy died of cancer. Lewis was alone again. But this aloneness was a thousandfold greater than before. In the months of grief that followed Joy's death, Lewis wrote one of the truly classic works about the grief experience. It was his personal journal later published as *A Grief Observed.* At a time when working was impossible and shaving required too much effort, Lewis wrote:

> Meanwhile, where is God?...When you are happy...and turn to Him with gratitude and praise, you will be—or so it feels—welcomed with open arms. But go to Him when your need is desperate, when all other help is vain, and what do you find? A door slammed in your face, and a sound of bolting and double bolting on the inside. After that, silence. You may as well turn away. The longer you wait, the more emphatic the silence will become.[4]

Silence from behind the double bolting door. The silence from a house where there are no lights in the windows.

"Was it ever inhabited?" Lewis pondered. "It seemed so once."[5]

God's silence troubled Lewis in his time of grief. That silence always frightens me. Yes, there have been occasions when the silence of God has caused me to question the existence of God. In such times I have felt like the night rider in Walter de le Mare's poem:

> "Is anybody there?" said the Traveler,
> Knocking on the moonlit door;
> And his horse in the silence champed the grasses
> Of the forest's ferny floor;
> And a bird flew up out of the turret,
> Above the Traveler's head:
> And he smote upon the door again a second time;
> "Is anybody there?" he said.
> But no one descended to the Traveler;
> No head from the leaf-fringed sill
> Leaned over and looked into his gray eyes,
> Where he stood perplexed and still.[6]

Is anybody there?

When Lewis hurt most, he felt the most alone. He felt the house of life was empty. If anyone was at home, the tenant was not acknowledging callers. I, too, have had moments when I questioned the existence of God. I know I am not alone in my doubts.

Is anyone there?

If so, what can I expect from Him or Her when I pound on the door in my moment of desperate need?

Unfortunately, it is not that easy for me—to just stop believing. Disbelief comes easy when God is absent in my moments of great need. But if God does not exist, why are there times when I feel God's presence in a way that defies disbelief? Lewis was far more honest and accurate than I when he spoke of the silence:

> Not that I am (I think) in much danger of ceasing to believe in God. The real danger is of coming to believe such dreadful things about Him. The conclusion I dread is not 'So there's no God after all,' but 'So this is what God's really like. Deceive yourself no longer.'[7]

And Thomas asks, *"Chaplain, where was God when I was raped?"*

In my earliest training at home and at church, I was taught that God is all-loving, all-powerful, all-knowing, and ever-present. I grew up believing in the words of David, that if the Lord is my shepherd I would not want for anything I needed (Ps 23). I believed God was my shepherd and I wanted for very little. I did not face the gripping fear of some great evil; goodness and mercy have followed me most of the days of my life.

In this kind of soil the so-called "prosperity Gospel" can easily take root. The notion that life is an endless system of rewards and punishments is a perversion of the Christian message. There have always been those who proclaim faith and goodness as the blue chip investment that guarantees success and prosperity. In nearly every generation someone rediscovers this idea and parades it like a newly discovered law of the universe. But it is not new. It is, in fact, as old as *homo sapiens.*

The Hebrew scriptures are well marked with road signs that warn about this kind of assumed guarantee. The chronicles of the kings boldly note that Manasseh was one of the worst kings to occupy the throne of Judah, and Josiah one of the finest. Yet it was Manasseh who had a long and peaceful reign of fifty-five years. Josiah was cut down in battle as a young man of forty (Cf. 2 Kgs 21:1-18; 22:1-20; 23:29).

The notion that the righteous are always rewarded and the wicked do not escape punishment is as popular today as in the days of the great prophets of Israel. However, to hold onto this view is to ignore the massive warning of the book of Job. The author of Job insists that the opposite is often true. The good are not always rewarded. The innocent are not immune to loss. The good and the innocent—they too get raped!

Believing in good and God does not make everything in life good and godly. If you do not already realize that bad things do happen to good people, read the Book of Job. If you are still not convinced, ask your next door neighbor.

> *"Where was God when I was raped?"* Thomas asked. *"What was he doing?"*

Thomas's words created intolerable images in my mind. At first I imagined God in the heavens, sitting on a throne inlaid with gold and pearls. Angels singing glory and praise encircled the throne while down below a washrag is stuffed into a child's mouth to muffle his cries while he is raped. Worse yet were thoughts of God standing at the foot of that child's bed, watching—just watching.

Lewis is right. It is not the danger of ceasing to believe in the existence of God that I have battled; at times I think it would be simpler and easier if there were no God. The real task of faith is to face the discovery of what God is really like.

The question many are coming to terms with today is not whether the Bible is true or whether we can believe what the Bible teaches us about God. Rather, it is the challenge of scholars like Dr. Kenneth E. Bailey, professor of New Testament with the Near East School of Theology in Beruit, Lebanon, to "examine our individual and collective traditions of interpreting the Bible—in light of the Bible."[8] There is a true sense in which each generation must return to the Bible and prayerfully reconsider their way of understanding the Bible. This needs to be done in light of the expanding knowledge we have about biblical events and customs and the significance of the methods ancient authors used in their efforts to communicate their experiences of God.

Is God a powerful and good supreme eternal Father who, at times, stands there and does nothing while evil tramples gleefully over innocent boys and girls, men and women—his children?

As a congregational pastor, I have listened to many people question the meaning of sickness and tragedy in their lives. I have celebrated at births, shed a tear of joy at weddings and graduations, and cried at funerals. As a hospital chaplain, I spend many hours every week with people who rejoice and cry in response to every kind of life experience one can imagine. The questions are varied and many, but they all have a recurring theme. Each speaks of an underlying need to make some sense out of what has happened, to find a reason or some meaning in it.

Viktor Frankl suggests this is a primary factor in understanding human personality and behavior. Frankl developed an approach to psychotherapy that challenged Sigmund Freud's main assumption. Freud stressed frustration in what he identified as the sexual drive as the major root of neuroses. Frankl's harrowing experiences in the Nazi prison camps did not support Freud's view. Frankl saw a deeper psychological and theological basis for the human person. It was not natural instinct or sex drive that motivated people to live in the shadow of the gallows and the stench of the crematoriums. Frankl saw that in the darkest hours a person could find a sense of meaning to his or her life, no matter how slight or how dismal. He observed that the incredible capacity people have for finding meaning is not in the circumstances they face. It is within themselves. Frankl found that people could survive the most inhumane circumstances if they were in touch with a *will-to-meaning*. These people, Frankl discovered, remained human beings. They did not become animals or mere zombies. Perhaps what Frankl identified as a will-to-meaning is but the twin brother of the sisters, faith and hope. Could this be but another way of naming what we really mean when we say God?

Frankl stressed frustration in the will-to-meaning as the underlying root of the distress and disorders in human personality. It is this will-to-meaning that enables people to survive. Frankl used the term logotherapy to designate this approach to psychotherapy. Logotherapy is the therapy of meaning. Frankl believed that a person who has a *why* to live can bear with almost any *how*.[9]

Behind the questions we ask about suffering and evil is the desire to find some meaning in what we are experiencing. If we can make some sense out of it, we are able to say, "I can accept it or at least handle it." When we find some meaning or possible good coming out of a tragedy, it gives us a sense of control over it and it reassures us that there is a rationale to life. It suggests there are secrets to living and, if discovered, they will give us a way to manipulate the forces and events of life.

In a civilization shaped by two world wars, Korea, Vietnam, the Gulf Crisis, apartheid and the ever-present potential of nuclear annihilation, the value of meaning is intensified. Our quest for the secrets to secure living becomes more urgent. With all of this we become more acutely aware of the lack of control we have over our world and our lives. How are we to live in a world so shaped by evil? It is not only individual tragedy that brings us face to face with Thomas's question (most of us have never been raped), but his question is echoed in the very atmosphere of our world. This is one reason the question is so automatic to victims. It is a question about meaning and purpose.

It is important, however, to remember that the first note sounded in a why question is a basic expression of despair. It is not a request for information. On the surface it is not a deep theological or philosophical question; it is simply an expression of shock and anguish. Experienced counselors know that the first response to this cry of a victim's lamentations should follow the example of Job's illustrative three friends—Eliphaz, Zophar, and Bildad. Hearing of Job's troubles, they went to visit him. For seven days and seven nights they sat with him in his anguish. They did not talk; they just sat and listened to his lamentations (Jb 2:11-13). They seemed to understand that Job was deeply hurt, that he needed to cry and be sad. To ask "why" is one way to express the unspeakable pain and sadness felt in the aftermath of tragedy. Paul Tillich noted this when he spoke of the "why" kind of question. Such a question does not make a request for information; it is an expression of one's "state of existence rather than a...formulated question."10

Tillich calls the state of existence expressed in the question of why a "state of estrangement." This sense of estrangement indicates some level of awareness that one is estranged from others and self— and from God. It is the fearful realization that one is impotent and alone before the forces and events of life. In such moments, whoever one trusted and believed would provide the needed protection is not coming through as expected.

Often in times of great difficulty our secret hope that God will treat us special, protect us, or let us get away with something un-punished is called to account. When the earth tilts suddenly and we lose our footing, we face the core of who we are and what we believe about the meaning of life—about God.

The cry of "why" is not a bad question, but many people feel guilty when they question the bad things that happen in life. They perceive questioning as a lack of faith, even an act of rebellion. How-ever, not to question is a sign of fatalism rather than a sign of faith. It limits the possibilities within a dynamic faith.

For the Christian, the most poignant example of appropriate ques-tioning when bad things happen is recorded in Mark 15:34. The Gos-pel gives us the final words of Jesus as he died. The scene is outside the city wall of Jerusalem. Three crosses are there. Jesus is hanging on the center cross. Mark notes that shortly before his death, Jesus is overcome with anguish and calls out to God, "E'loi, E'loi, la'ma sa-bachtha'ni? My God, My God, why have you forsaken me?"[11] Are we to take Jesus' words seriously? Can we believe that Jesus meant what he said? If we do, we must hear the despair, pain, and perhaps fear that every person experiences who feels utterly abandoned and powerless in the face of tragedy or the impact of evil.

Jesus' words clarify the intensity of his physical suffering. At the same time they raise a serious and confusing problem; namely, is Jesus simply expressing human surprise and anguish at his situation, or is he actually asking a question about purpose: "God, why have you done this?" Is Jesus possibly speaking of a more pressing con-cern—a concern closely akin to that of Thomas—the concern of *re-lationship* and *availability*?

Jesus is not asking about the reason for his death. He had worked this out over the three prior years. It was only a firm understanding of the reason and meaning of his death that enabled him to face it. Jesus had a close and trusting relationship with God. That trust served well his need for meaning in life. Nevertheless, in his moment of greatest tragedy, Jesus encounters something about God that even he evidently had not fully experienced or understood: the absence of God.

On deeper analysis, Jesus' question becomes a question of re-lationship—proximity and availability. Awakened by the full force of human brutality, it is a natural and real response. But it is also a response, from the core of his being, about the meaning of his life and his relationship with God.

C. S. Lewis understood Jesus' words. Jesus was not seeking information about reasons for all that was happening. Jesus, as did Lewis, wanted to know where God was. Both Lewis and Jesus felt God's presence when life was good. But in their individual hour of greatest need they had a grave question about God's availability to them. They are in anguish. They cry out. God is somewhere—but not with them. There is a feeling—a fear—that the relationship has changed! The silence that haunted Lewis when he called out to God at the time of Joy's death also perplexed Jesus. Jesus was actually questioning God's availability to him. Jesus was inquiring as to the Eternal's whereabouts. If Jesus knew who he was and understood his relationship with God, the question "why" is meaningless. The only question that holds any meaning for Jesus as he is crucified is "where." *Where* is God?

Jesus must have felt keenly the absence of God, the silence of the non-presence of God—the silence from behind Lewis's closed and double bolted door. That was a mystery even to Jesus. That caught him off guard. A more accurate rendering of his question might be:

> *"My God, my God, I am dying. Where are you?"*

These words are similar to those of Job during the hours when he felt God had abandoned him (Jb 3:20-23). Every person who suffers injustice and wrong faces these feelings. In Job's case, evil raped almost everything he cherished in life. The only thing he did not lose was his wife and his life. Job could not make any sense out of it. What wrong had he done to merit such treatment? Worse yet, Job felt God had abandoned him in the moment of his tragedy. Job, as Jesus and Lewis, beseeched God from the silence of his abandonment.

> *"Where was God when I was raped?"* asked Thomas.
> *"Where was God when I lost my wealth and my health?"* asked Job.
> *"Where was God's protection when I was slain on the battlefield?"* asked Josiah.
> *"Where was God when I lost my wife?"* asked Lewis.
> *"My God, my God, where are you?"* asked Jesus.

Rabbi Kushner's book, *When Bad Things Happen to Good People,* addresses the "why" question from the Judaic view of scripture and tradition. Rabbi Kushner, as did I, likely learned many answers to these kinds of questions in the seminary. But what we learned had to be tested out in our experiences with flesh-and-blood people in moments of untimely, enigmatic suffering and death. Rabbi Kushner states: "I knew...that one day I would write this book. I would write it out of my own need to put into words some of the most important things I have come to believe and know."[12] At the age of three, Rabbi Kushner's son, Aaron, had been diagnosed as having a rare and fatal disease. Aaron died in his early teens. Kushner writes: "There is only one question which really matters: why do bad things happen to good people?"[13] Why is this the one and only question that matters? Frankl suggested it is because of the human *will-to-meaning*—the need to make sense out of what happens to us. We weave the fabric of meaning to clothe our lives from what we believe about what happens to us.

Rabbi Kushner's message is clear. God does not send the bad and tragic things that happen to us. This is important. We will consider ramifications of this in later pages. However, for the Thomases of life, Kushner passes over the central concern. It is reassuring to know that God has not singled me out to experience pain or suffering. But if I am to trust God and look to God for help when such things do come, I want to know where God is and what God is doing during my plight. Is God with me in this?

Author Philip Yancey and many others suggest that at such times I must trust God's higher level of purpose in my suffering. My suffering is a help to God in accomplishing something I do not know about. Job is offered as an example. Job was special because he was chosen to suffer for God's higher good—God's need to win his wager with Satan. My belief that God is making use of my suffering in some cosmic battle should make me feel special.

In Psalm 121 the psalmist writes:

> I will lift up mine eyes to the hills;
> from where does my help come?
> My help comes from the Lord,
> the maker of heaven and earth.

If we let the psalm say what it actually says, we discover that the author does not indicate that his pain or trouble comes from the Lord. Rather, he insists that his *help* comes from the Lord. If the psalmist's difficulties did come from the Lord, it would be a paradox or, worse, an absurdity—God sends pain to send relief; sends problems to send solutions; sends distress to send peace of mind.

I do not expect to find answers to my many questions nor to achieve certainty about all the issues of God, good, and evil. I am convinced, though, that God does not decide which parents will give birth to a handicapped child. God did not single out my high school friend to die of a brain tumor while the rest of us went on to college, nor did he select Kay, a mother of three, to die of cancer before she was thirty.

Rabbi Kushner agrees that God does not single out people to suffer and die. He is confident that we are not alone in trying times. In fact, God stands by ready to help.

Does God really stand by ready to help? Is that what we are up against—a God that helps after the fact? The idea of God coming to our aid after it is all over is as distressing as the assumption that God caused the situation to begin with. This is why Thomas's question is so relevant and inescapable. It calls for a clarification on how God is related to us at any given moment.

When I am in trouble I want to know where God stands on the issue and where God is when it is happening. What is God's relationship to me?

I would not be consoled or encouraged if someone stood by watching me be raped and did not speak a word or lift a finger to help me. Such a person would either be powerless to help or grossly insensitive and a coward. I could understand the powerlessness, but the latter...?

What kind of friend—or what kind of father—stands by and watches bad things happen and does nothing?

If you stand by and watch while I am raped, if you could help me and yet choose to do nothing, I do not want you to come after it is all over and offer help. In a moment like that, your assurances of your "love" for me would be meaningless. Your efforts to comfort me would be worthless. I would prefer that you remain silent and continue to do nothing. Above all else—don't you dare touch me!

Some readers may be wearied with questions. Others may be baffled. Is there really a difference between asking "Where is God when bad things happen?" and "Why do bad things happen?" Does it actually matter?

Does the answer to where God is offer anything different to the "Jobs" of life? I believe it does. The answer to "why" gives reasons and offers justification for God's silence or inaction. The quest for "where" God is in those moments lets us know how God is involved in what is happening.

Moché the Beadle once told Elie Wiesel that every question possesses a power that does not lie in the answer. Wiesel tells of his relationship with Moché in his monumental little book *Night*.[14] Moché was from a poor family in Elie's village. He was awkward and the town clown. He made people laugh, but no one took him seriously. However, it was Moché who offered to guide his young friend Elie in the study of the cabbala[15] when others told him he was too young.

During one of their long discussions, Moché and Elie talked about the power and purpose of questions. Moché said: "Man raises himself toward God by the questions he asks Him. This is the true dialogue. Man questions God and God answers. But we don't understand His answers. We can't understand them. Because they come from the depths of the soul…You will find the true answers, Eliezer, only within yourself!"[16]

Why do bad things happen to people is a legitimate and powerful question. Rabbi Kushner and others have examined a variety of answers people offer to this age-old question. Some of these same reasons for suffering surfaced that day in the spiritual values group. These were not the answers Thomas was seeking. But, as is often the case, these were the answers the group focused on.

And to be candid, for a while, I was glad they did.

NOTES

1. Earnest Jones, "Psycho-analysis and the Christian Religion," *Essays in Applied Psychoanalysis,* Vol. 11 (London: Hogart Press, Ltd., 1951), p. 302.

2. Paul W. Pruyser, *The Minister as Diagnostician* (Philadelphia: The Westminister Press, 1976), p. 64.

3. *The Living Bible* (Wheaton, Illinois: Tyndale House Publishers, Inc., 1971). "How long, O Lord, will you look on," New Revised Standard Version.

4. C. S. Lewis, *A Grief Observed* (New York: Bantam Books, Inc., 1976), p. 5.

5. *Ibid.,* p. 5.

6. Walter de le Mare, *The Listeners.*

7. Lewis, *op. cit.,* p. 5.

8. Kenneth E. Bailey, Lecture Series, Linfield College (McMinnville, Oregon, Summer 1990).

9. Viktor Frankl, *Man's Search for Meaning* (Boston: Beacon Press, 1963), pp. x-xi.

10. Paul Tillich, *The Courage to Be* (New Haven, Connecticut: Yale University Press, 1952), pp. 59ff.

11. *egkataleipw.* Literally, "to leave in a place or situation; to leave behind, to abandon. *Analytical Greek Lexicon* (Grand Rapids, Michigan: Zondervan Publishing House, 1978), p. 113.

12. Harold S. Kushner, *When Bad Things Happen to Good People* (New York: Schocken Books, 1981), p. 4.

13. *Ibid.*, p. 6.

14. Elie Wiesel, *Night* (New York: Bantam Books, 1986), p. 2.

15. *Cabbala:* the study of the world of the Jewish mystics; normally studied when a man was in his thirties.

16. Wiesel, *op. cit.*, p. 3.

CHAPTER TWO

THE PERPLEXITY:
Wrong Questions,
Wrong Answers

It was very warm in the group room. I glanced quickly at my watch as I loosened my tie. Fifteen minutes had passed. It seemed like an hour.

> *"You reap what you sow,"* Susan reminded us, recalling a Bible verse from her childhood.
> *"Yeah, remember what happened to Adam and Eve,"* another suggested with a laugh that brought momentary relief from the strained atmosphere pervading the group.
> *"Chaplain, do you believe there really was an Adam and Eve?"* someone asked.
> I was tempted to talk about Genesis and creation....

Many people have sincere questions about the biblical description of creation. Some see in it a literal description of the way God created the universe. God said "I want apples" and suddenly they were hanging on a tree fully ripe and ready to eat.

> *"That's the way it happened, isn't it, Chaplain? I believe it word for word. Don't you?"*

Is the Genesis story intended to be a historical accounting of the way it happened or is it an inspired and true message about the meaning of what happened? I believe the message of the Genesis story is true. It is a message about the God who caused the universe as we know it. Of greater importance, however, is the Genesis meaning. It

25

tells us how God is related to the creation and its creatures—to us.

The God of my childhood made the world in much the same way as I made mud pies and sand castles in my backyard: molding, shaping, destroying by whim and will. But those childhood images no longer fit my experiences in the front yards and on the freeways of adulthood. Paul notes this kind of idea as he closes his great discourse on love: "When I was a child, I spoke like a child, I thought like a child, I reasoned like a child; when I became a man, I gave up childish ways" (1 Cor 13:11).

This is often part of the emotional dilemma of many people. Their image of God was formed when they were children. At that age black and white thinking is natural and works well in a child's world. Childhood is also a time of unlimited imagination, an imagination that is undaunted by the dynamic complexities and interrelated actualities of life. The world of adult experience, on the other hand, is not black and white. The adult world is made up of many colors and an endless variation of shades.

In a child's world, two plus two always equals four. As we grow older, knowledge expands and our understanding changes. We learn about minus and plus numbers: minus-two plus two equals zero. We discover that the impossible is easy. A person walking up and another person walking down are going in opposite directions, but they can easily reach the same spot in the same moment.

In adulthood, we discover that the world is complex. One person's single action becomes a chain reaction that many experience. Yet, often, we attempt to make adult experiences fit the images and understanding of God we formed as a child. Those images and comprehensions served us well as children. But they no longer fit our adult world/life view nor match our level of perception of reality. Those childhood images helped build a foundation for the demands of a mature faith, but we cannot live as an adult with images we built out of knowledge from childhood. Nevertheless, this is precisely what many sincere and well-intentioned people try to do. They try to calculate a formula for plotting the future movement of a planet by using introductory geometry and a plastic protractor.

"Chaplain, don't you?" Mary repeated. She was frustrated that I didn't seem to hear her question.

I did hear Mary. At the moment, a discussion about the Genesis story was more appealing than Thomas's question.

I sidestepped the new question and tried to focus again on Thomas. He did not realize it, but he was challenging us to look at the underlying concern of Genesis. The message of Genesis from "the beginning," whenever it was and however it came about, is that God and humanity are inseparably and intimately involved. God not only caused the world to begin but God has also been involved in every facet of its development from that beginning.

"That's a fair question," I replied, *"but let's stay with Thomas's question a little longer. Do you think Adam and Eve's experience tells us anything about Thomas's question?"*

The group became silent.

"Susan is right," I said. *"One thing we must face in life is the fact that we are prone 'to reap what we sow.' Does that relate to Thomas's question, 'Where was God when I was raped?' "*

The group ignored my effort to refocus on Thomas's question. As the discussion continued, I did not emphasize Susan's point about "sowing and reaping." Many persons with chronic or acute emotional problems are often overburdened with sins and shortcomings. They are quick to claim full responsibility for the bad things that happen to them. Refusing to accept responsibility for one's thoughts and actions is often a significant part of anxiety and more serious emotional problems; the opposite is often the case. Frequently, depression and other emotional distresses are, at least in part, the consequences of a person's refusal to acknowledge that someone else is responsible for the bad stuff that has happened to them.

I continue to be amazed at the load of inappropriate guilt many people carry around, a guilt about things and events for which they are not responsible. Most of us have enough guilt that is rightfully our own without assuming the responsibility and guilt that belong to someone else.

People are often surprised when I accuse them of stealing guilt. That is precisely what happens when a person feels guilty or responsible for something someone else did. This is inherent in the makeup of victims of incest. They take possession of the guilt and evil that belongs only to the perpetrator. This was one hopeful sign about Thomas. He was beginning to accept the truth that someone else was to blame for all that happened to him as a child.

The reference to Adam and Eve was made partly in jest in an effort to ease the anxiety in the group. But the Genesis account of the beginning of human experience does illustrate the age-old explanation of why bad things happen to people. The answer is simple. They deserve it.

The Book of Genesis tells us God evicted Adam and Eve from the Garden of Eden, cursed with a sinful nature because of their willful disobedience. God instructed them not to eat the fruit from the tree of knowledge of good and evil, yet they ate the forbidden fruit. They were disobedient. When people misbehave, bad things happen to them. For many people it is that simple. Do good and receive a reward. Do bad and you are punished. Two plus two equals four. It is a matter of cause and effect.

I don't find it easy to accept the consequences of my folly or sin. I suspect few people do. When we choose to break the law, take a chance, commit a sin, none of us has a legitimate gripe when we suffer the consequences of our choices. They are our choices and our responsibilities. The complaint that someone else did the same thing and got away with it is really beside the point. However, in such times the question, "Where is God?" is not important. In truth, when I choose to do something wrong, I want to think God is not near. I secretly hope God chooses to go fishing on those days.

How can a person apply the concept of cause and effect and personal responsibility to Thomas's situation? I could not do it. If I accept the "cause-effect" answer for the bad things that happen, I am still out on a limb trying to understand the abuse of people who are innocent of any complicity. To blame Thomas for the perverted cruelty he experienced is inappropriate. To make Thomas responsible in any way for the sexual perversion he experienced is as sick as the perversion itself.

Time passed slowly; the group was handling the tenseness surprisingly well. A few more persons spoke, but with hesitation.

"I've always thought that everything that happens to us will make us better people...kind of like God is trying to make us grow or something," Mary said. It was not clear whether she

was asking a question or making a statement.

*"I've been told that all of my life—and that is why I'm here.
God is trying to teach me something right now,"* Bill added. *"I
hope I somehow find out what it is that God wants me to learn.
I'm thick-headed and God has to hit me up side of the head now
and then to get my attention."*

Once again there was laughter. I cringed at the idea of God
going around hitting people "up side of the head." I felt sick in
the pit of my stomach because there are many like Bill who
think of God as some kind of redneck who demonstrates love
by being cruel.

This is the second most common reason people give to explain the
bad things that happen to us; that is, suffering will purge us and
make us better persons. I hoped no one in the group would mention
this idea. I have heard too often these insensitive words spoken to
suffering persons.

It is true. Many people discover good aspects of themselves in suffering. To turn tragedy or a wrong into an opportunity to change and
to grow in character and wisdom is a marvelous accomplishment. Almost everyone knows someone who has done this. These folks are
sources of inspiration to our world and give testimony to the power
of what Frankl calls the "defiant human spirit." They reveal a capacity to overcome great odds. They give observable evidence of a vital
faith, a faith par excellence. It is a faith in God, in others, and in
themselves that frees the power and zest for living in a way that
defies and alters human boundaries. It is a faith that supersedes and
transforms circumstances. But does it follow that this is the purpose
of tragedy and the reason for suffering?

Standing on the sidelines of another's situation and announcing
that the sufferer must accept their plight because it is God's way of
purging him or her from some personality defect or spiritual short-
coming is to make judgments beyond human right or capacity. The
Bible is filled with admonitions against such judgmental declarations
(e.g., Mt 7:1-5; Lk 6:37ff).

The chaplain was making "pre op" visits to patients scheduled for
surgery the next day. When she entered the pediatric unit, she saw a
mother she had visited earlier. She was obviously upset. The mother
told the chaplain that the treatment for her little girl was not proving

effective. The child was dangerously ill. The mother could hardly bear to see her daughter in such excruciating pain. She talked of the family's faith and their confusion. "Why was God doing this?" Earlier in the afternoon her daughter asked, "Mommy, God isn't taking very good care of me, is he?"

Wiping away her tears, the mother added, "Chaplain, I didn't answer her. I just stroked her forehead. How do you explain to a child that God sends these things?"

How do you explain to a child—or anyone else—that God sends these things? I can't because I don't believe that is true. I would rather face life without God than to live with the thought that God is so insensitive to human experience that immeasurable pain and suffering are divinely prescribed treatments for the evil in the hearts and actions of five-year-old girls.

Many also believe that the future life is God's major concern. What happens in this life is of consequence only as it affects one's going to heaven or hell. I am acquainted with the anxieties that the future can excite. The idea of an eternity—an endless experience of timeless existence in a state of peace or pain—is a valid concern. But is God so future-oriented, so focused on a future state of heavenly bliss, that what happens today to a five-year-old girl does not matter and is only an inconsequential passing necessity?

There are some who note the impact that the suffering of a child has on the adults around her. As noted in chapter one, many claim that God uses such events to bring an unfaithful father, a worldly mother, or an alcoholic uncle to change their ways and get right with God.

The need for these changes is not the question. The question centers on Divine integrity. The method one uses to accomplish a goal speaks of the person's character. Does God hold innocent children hostage to pain and tragic suffering or the evil actions of others to bring some rebellious, sinful adult to repent? If this is true, C.S. Lewis is correct: There is grave reason to fear what we may discover about the nature of God in the moments of silence amid tragic and evil events.

Are we only chess pieces of relative value—usable and expendable—in some supreme chess game that God is playing with the devil?

I don't remember, but I think it was also Mary who asked,

"Chaplain, doesn't it say in the Bible that God won't let us be put through more than we can bear? (Sigh) *I just wish I was as strong as God expected me to be. My pastor keeps telling me to have more faith because God will make a way for me out of my troubles. If I just have more faith."*

Before I could reflect on my response, I blurted out, *"Mary, I have always been uncomfortable with that idea."*

To tell a person who is falling apart to have more faith, that God won't let her lose it, puts a person in a hopeless double bind. How does it help Mary for her to think that God is only testing her and won't let her be pushed beyond her breaking point? She is already past the breaking point. This kind of encouragement merely compounds the despair and guilt. It helps only the person who says it. Somehow it is easier for us to see others suffer if we can assure ourselves that God will, in some way, take care of them. After all, isn't it their fault that they went too far?

Mary already feels guilty and down on herself for the crisis she's in. Mary is getting assurance that it is her fault that she has broken under her burdens. God measured Mary's load and made sure it was not more than she could carry. "Shame on you, Mary, you broke too soon. You could have borne up under a lot more!"

"Mary," I continued, *"that kind of advice reminds me of a cartoon I saw on the bulletin board around here. It pictured a psychiatrist shouting at a nervous, upset patient, 'Relax! Relax! Relax!'"*

Once again the humor eased the strain for the moment.

"Mary, I really do not believe God puts burdens on us."

I have heard well-meaning people offer this idea repeatedly in an effort to bring meaning to bad times. It is meant as a token of encouragement and hope. I have seen people use this notion as a knot to hold onto when they were at the end of their rope. But when a person is caught in the cement mixer of anxiety and pain—or worse—this kind of advice is, I believe, theologically and psychologically unsound. In the effort to offer spiritual and psychological help, we must channel the help in a way that accepts and values the feelings and reality of the person's experience. They need help to move beyond the feelings to faith and new choices/actions, to ways of altering their

31

understanding and response to their reality. Admonitions that only compound guilt and a sense of failure are poor substitutes for the love and encouragement that the person needs.

In dealing with overpowering feelings, it is important to understand that faith is not a matter of feelings. There are times when I feel God is against me; God has abandoned me. It is true; that is the way I feel. The challenge? Can I choose to face what I am feeling at the present moment with what I believe to be true at other moments? During the dark hours I must wrestle with what I am feeling in opposition to what I have chosen to believe. Faith and feelings are not synonyms. The core of what one believes must be a commitment to faith, not feelings.

The examples of faith in the Scriptures deal with thought or action based on what people *believed* in spite of what they *felt*. Belief about God rather than feelings about God governed their attitude or action. Faith has never been a matter of feeling or fact. Faith is the mysterious dynamic that enables one to overcome feelings. Faith keeps a person from being totally limited by facts. The essence and meaning of faith is the capacity to live empowered by a relationship with "something" or "someone" in whom I believe, regardless of what I know by fact or accept by feeling. For me, that someone is God.

The author of the Letter to the Hebrews offers a truly inspired definition of faith: "Now faith is the assurance of things hoped for, the conviction of things not seen" (11:1).

Many people equate faith with a super insurance policy. Having faith assures them that life will be good. They have nothing to be concerned about as long as they "have faith." Their faith will protect them from bad things. Consequently, when bad things happen it is an indictment or a failure of faith, or possibly a citation for the kind of faith that merits testing.

Actually, the reverse is true. An insurance policy doesn't protect us from anything. Insurance doesn't keep bad things from happening. It merely compensates for losses from floods or fires or accidents. Insurance provides resources to enable us to find ways to rebuild or replace what has been lost or destroyed. This, likewise, is a major function of faith. Faith is the assurance and conviction that we can face anything that does—or does not—happen to us and still go on living by that faith.

Even Job needs little faith when his children have shiny faces and his herds are fat from a bountiful harvest. C.S. Lewis found God very near when his wife, Joy, was alive and with him. Such faith is easy and natural. It is not an issue when good things are happening. When life is good and even my competition votes for me as "Rotarian of the year," it is easy to trust in the goodness of the Almighty. (I secretly acknowledge that good done to me is always evidence of the Almighty's wisdom!)

Everyone can understand the logic that says good guys always win in the end. This is the simple logic of every child. Smile and coo and someone holds you. Cry and fret and you get a slap. Do your chores and you can play. Forget your chores and pay the consequences. Cause and effect, action with purpose. Most of us can handle this. Because of this kind of primitive reasoning, we base much of our belief about God on a retribution theology; that is, on the understanding that God rewards good behavior and punishes the bad. This kind of relationship, simple and clear, gives us a degree of control. If we do good, God will bless us. If we do bad, God will punish. Work hard and you will succeed. Don't try and you'll fail.

But when things get out of the prescribed order, we don't like it. We become confused and have doubts. We need faith precisely at these times of confusion and doubt. When things get out of order, that faith becomes essential for survival. Those are the times for filing a claim on our faith. Only a Job of faith can survive when the faces of his children are pale and stiff in death, his herds are bloated from starvation, and his fields are barren. That was the time when Job's faith was transformed from a policy guarantee he kept filed away to an actual resource for meaning and hope amidst despair.

No doubt Mary's pastor wanted to be encouraging when he instructed her to "have more faith and try harder." His notion that God would not allow her to have more trouble than she could handle did just the opposite. Rather than comfort her, it made her feel guilty for not being strong enough to keep herself from breaking. She now became down on herself for being so weak and thought God was displeased with her because she failed to stop short of her breaking point.

What the pastor told Mary is not true. The Bible does not teach such an idea. First Corinthians (10:13) is the common proof text for the notion that God will not put more on a person than he or she can bear. It reads:

No temptation has overtaken you that is not common to man. God is

33

faithful and he will not let you be tempted beyond your strength, but with the temptation will also provide the way of escape, that you may be able to endure it.[1]

People often quote this verse in an effort to offer comfort or challenge during hard times. It is usually misquoted, something like "Remember, God won't put more on you than you can bear." A greater travesty is that it is misapplied. It is a reference to a person's being tempted to sin. It has no reference to the things that happen to us in life when we do not have a choice. The context of this notion does not address the subject of tragedies or the actions of evil taken against an innocent person.

Paul was writing to the people of first-century Corinth about the inner workings of temptation. Paul describes several types of behavior and activities in which some of the Corinthian Christians were evidently involved. Paul addresses the matter of one's responsibility for his or her immoral behavior. He notes that it is normal to be tempted to do wrong. It is part of the human condition, as he points out in some of his other writings (see Romans 7). The word Paul uses in Corinthians for temptation is *peirasmos*. It is a word used in the New Testament to signify an enticement to sin, a lure to do something contrary to the Law of God.[2] When a person is tempted to do wrong, the response comes from within the person. The context seems to suggest that some people claimed that God caused them to sin. Their logic went like this: "God made me and I am the way I am because of divine creation. My desires, my needs are God's fault. The potter cannot condemn the pot for being what the potter made it to be."

This kind of thinking was offensive to Paul. He assures his readers that they—not God—are responsible for their own actions. If you sin, Paul says, it is your fault, not God's! Paul does not agree with the view made notoriously popular by the comedian Flip Wilson's Geraldine, "The devil made me do it!" In this passage Paul is precise; if I do wrong it is because *I* made me do it.

But Paul offers encouragement to his readers when he assures them that God is ultimately in control. God will not allow them to be tempted to do wrong beyond their strength to resist. These few words seem to turn theological thinking back to the days of Job. In an effort to defend God against the claim that people are the way they are because God made them that way, Paul all but proves that very claim.

If God will not allow me to be tempted to do wrong beyond the point where I can resist the urge to do it, then the unavoidable conclusion is that every temptation in some way is under God's control. If God has any degree of control over our temptations, then we draw one of two conclusions.

First, God is directly sending the temptations. If God sends them, then it would seem logical that God would also send our tragedies. Thus, we envision God as manipulating circumstances and people to align them for the right conditions to create a bad situation. God is off somewhere deciding, "I think I will put Horace in a compromising situation where he will be so besieged that he will be all but driven to...."

Second, God is not responsible for sending our temptations, but is in control of them. That is, God could keep temptations from occurring but does not choose to prevent them. God does not protect me from temptations but maintains control over the boundaries and limits of my temptations.

As in the story of Job, Satan comes to God and gets permission to tempt me. So Job's Satan comes to God and says, "You know Horace Duke, one of your small-time pastoral counselors down there on earth. He feels rather secure about the way his work has gone over the years. He's never gotten out of line with a counselee. Big deal! You and I both know that's only because you are nice to him. You never let me push him to his limit. Now if you just let me...."

Hearing the demonic request, God says, "Go ahead, tempt him and give him problems. Do all sorts of things to him. You can put his accounts in arrears. You can cancel his membership in all those 'alphabet clubs'—ACPE, GCC, C of C, AMFC. You can give him shin splints from jogging. Tempt him with blondes and redheads, old women and young ones, women with short hair and long hair—even gray hair. But no brunettes. You have to stop short of brunettes—especially brunettes over fifty with blue-green eyes. He just couldn't resist that temptation."

Such a dialogue sounds absurd, demeaning, even blasphemous—except in the prologue to the Book of Job (a section that scholars conclude was added by a different writer years after the completion of the main text). This idea makes God somewhat of a co-conspirator with the persons and forces of wrong and evil. If not a co-conspirator with evil, at least an agency to license the "evil one." Under this notion, any agent of temptation would be authorized to function with a license that the Department of Divine Providence issued. This logic, as in the prologue to the Book of Job, makes the winds of tragedy and the brutes of evil agents of God's licensee. There is a sense where Satan, in the Book of Job, sees himself as a quality inspector hired, as it were, to check on one of God's workers.

This raises several critical problems. I will address these in chapter four. But as I faced Thomas's agony, I began to see these thoughts for what they are. They are clearly distortions of who God is and how God relates to us when we are victims of the tragic and the evil we are not responsible for.

If we understand tragic and evil events as a means for God to test us, we cast God in a strange and paradoxical role. It is to say that a Divine end justifies an evil or less than good means. If God knows our breaking points in any kind of temptation or testing, then it is an unavoidable implication that we will not be pushed beyond our breaking point. The purpose of a test determines if we know certain things, can accomplish them, or demonstrate them. If God already knows, God does not need to put a person through suffering and loss to prove what Divine knowledge already knows. If this is true, then why the charade? Some quickly respond that the purpose is to prove a point. We will never know how strong we are or how well we can handle horrible things if we do not experience a few of them.

Tragedies are sent our way to test our strength. The logic goes like this. If I never have a fire in my home, I will never know how quickly the fire department responds, how skilled the firefighters are at putting out fires, or how good my insurance policy is. Using this logic, a fire would be a blessing and I should be grateful for it. Perhaps I should request one.

The question is not, should I cope with my tragedies and suffering, should I challenge myself to make sense out of what happens to me. To cope, to survive, to have any hope to go on living I must make sense out of what happens to me. Rather, the sticky point is *how* do I make sense out of a God who puts me through this kind of experience? *Where* is God when these things happen? *How* is God involved? The answer to these questions form the meaning I give to my experiences of good and bad. They tell me a great deal about God: the kind of relationship we have, what I can count on from God, how my faith and the power of God work together, the real intention of Divine Providence.

Her small, round face, filled with life, lighted up any room she entered. Her name? Vicki Lynn, my first-born child. It was a hot Thursday in July 1955. I was still enjoying the summer vacation from college. Hauling rock was hard work, but it was a summer job and hard work has a way of making a young man feel strong. The sweat on my back felt good in the occasional Arkansas breeze. Dr. Coppenger operated the rented bulldozer with extraordinary skill. We were loading rock we had dug earlier that morning. It was unusual to see him hot and sweaty in dirty jeans. As he sat astride the dozer, one would never have imagined him a professor of philosophy and religion. Only a few weeks earlier I sat in his class taking copious lecture notes. I felt special when he asked me to help him dig rock for the house he was building in the faculty village.

A few miles away in the student village we called "The Farm," Vicki was laughing and playing in her bed. She went to sleep for a nap but an hour later she was dead. Today we call it SIDS (Sudden Infant Death Syndrome). Dead at ten months of age. Stricken by God? Stricken with God's permission? Was this to make me see how strong I was? Or to discover how great my faith is under pressure? If that were the case, I guess I would have chosen not to know. I learned a great deal about life, myself, and my faith as I worked through that experience. So did Vicki's mother, grandparents, and other relatives and friends. A day finally came when I could recognize blessings in my coping with that tragic event. Our baby's death affected my life in some very positive ways. Ralph Waldo Emerson was right: "The years teach us much that the days never know." I went on living. I didn't give up on life, or people, or God. I had other children. But did God cause Vicki to die so I could learn those things? Were pain and suffering God's chosen way to teach us?

Archibald MacLeish expressed the strange nature of this logic in his Pulitzer Prize-winning play called *J.B.* The play, written in verse, is a contemporary version of the Book of Job. Two of the characters, Nickles and Mr. Zuss, discuss the ordeal of the original Job and ponder reasons why anyone should suffer. They suggest that Job's suffering is God's way to teach him about his need for God.

Nickles:	Why must he suffer then?
Mr. Zuss:	To praise!... He trusts God.
	No matter how it ends, he trusts Him.
Nickles:	Even when God tests him?— tortures him?
Mr. Zuss:	Would God permit the test unless

	He knew the outcome of the testing?
Nickles:	Then why test him if God knows?
Mr. Zuss:	So Job can see.
Nickles:	See what?
Mr. Zuss:	See God.
Nickles:	A fine sight from an ash heap, certainly!
Mr. Zuss:	Isn't there anything you understand?
	It's from the ash heap God is seen.
	Always! Always from the ashes.
	Every saint and martyr knew that.
Nickles:	And so he suffers to see God;
	Sees God because he suffers. Beautiful![3]

The group's comments were representative of the common explanations used to make sense out of suffering and unexplainable tragedy. The list is as varied as people and imagination. But one thing is clear about each answer. They all have a similar underlying concept. Rabbi Kushner noted this when he concluded that all the standard explanations as to why bad things happen to us have "at least one thing in common. They all assume that God is the cause..." God is either the direct cause or the indirect cause of the bad things that happen to us. These seem to be the only two options. God either does it or allows it! As Kushner considered this bad that happens to us, he pondered: "Is it for our own good, or is it a punishment we deserve, or could it be that God does not care what happens to us?"[4]

At the time of Vicki's death, many assured me that her death was for some yet unknown good, some unlearned lesson. Some people assured themselves that Vicki's death was punishment for a hidden sin. Either way, God did it. God allowed it for my good or caused it because I was bad. I am convinced neither of these is true. God's good or my bad did not cause Vicki's death. But if neither is true, what about Kushner's alternative? Could it really be true that God doesn't care what happens to us? This is disturbing. Some refuse to consider it. I wonder. Was David's psalm all about this? Was that David's fear—that God stood there and did nothing while he suffered because God did not care about what was happening to him?

I could live with the idea of a God who causes bad things for good reasons; even a God who causes good and bad capriciously. That would make God quite human. But the idea of a God who does not care one way or the other distresses me a great deal. And yet, what could David think? He prayed for help and none was forthcoming. What am I to think when a Tomahawk cruise missile armed with an atomic warhead seeks me out and explodes in the center of my world?

M. Scott Peck calls attention to the strange phenomenon often observed in victims of abuse. Peck terms this a "law of child development...specific to the problem of evil." He notes, "When a child is grossly confronted by significant evil in its parents, it will most likely misinterpret the situation and believe that the evil resides in itself."[5]

Beth was a teacher in a nearby university. She was working with a pastoral counselor to help her deal with issues of guilt and depression. She was plump, obviously overweight. Her youthful face was starkly clean; she wore no makeup. Her shoulder-length hair was clean but unkempt. She spoke in a soft voice with some hesitation. Her words were deliberate and concise. It was hard to imagine her in front of a university class teaching clinical psychology. Her doctorate gave her the opportunity to teach the subject she understood and loved, but it had not freed her from a burden of guilt and doubt.

It was a family secret. Beth was the victim of incest from the age of twelve until she left home after high school. At puberty she took on most of her mother's role in the family, including sleeping with her father. She and her father were inseparable and as a child she was a loner. Beth was a good student and was never a problem in school. She grew up assuming that all girls slept with their fathers. Not until she entered college did she begin to realize how different she was. After years of education and social interaction, Beth still blamed herself for the sexual abuse. She was the victim, but she saw it as her fault. As we gradually peeled back the layers of defensive scars, Beth began to come to terms with herself as the victim. To accept the fact that her father didn't care about her when he had sex with her was painful. Regardless of the reasons for his behavior, it was because of those reasons that he did not care! The driving desire to satisfy his own needs blocked his capacity to care about what he was doing to Beth.

As are many victims of incest, Beth was unable to experience anger and rage toward her father. Month after month she defended him in a variety of ways, always excusing him and blaming herself.

When clients tell me about the sexual abuse they endured, I often feel disgust and anger toward their abuser. Initially, I am bewildered at their inability to blame their fathers and uncles and brothers. Repeatedly, they blame themselves and, occasionally, their mothers. I often find it hard to contain my anger over the abuses clients talk about. I struggle to be patient and to aid them in their efforts to own the experiences and their repressed emotions toward their abusers.

Karen's story, although similar to Beth's, is worse. I was the first pastoral counselor to work with her. She had six prior therapists. Her father and an uncle sexually assaulted her as a child. For over twelve years she was forced repeatedly to have intercourse with her brothers. The incest and abuse included physical and emotional beatings that continued into her teens. It stopped when, with her own efforts, the court removed her from the home. The impact of such gross and continuous evil devastated Karen. It seemed we would never be able to redirect the anger and the rage from herself to those deserving it. It took years of therapy and pastoral work to begin dislodging the conviction Karen lived with. She believed she was a bottomless pit of "bad." She assumed full responsibility for the evil her family perpetrated on her. Taking the blame for the wrongs others had done to her was the way her childish mind could survive the ordeal. It was logical for her to assume, "They would not be doing those things to me if I didn't deserve it." The more they abused her, the more she was compelled to find reasons that she deserved it.

In my work as a chaplain, I discovered that this kind of thinking is not limited to children. Dr. Edward E. Thornton, professor of pastoral theology at Southern Baptist Theological Seminary, also made this observation in his ministry to hospital patients:

> I am impressed by the tenacious way many patients hold that the meaning of their illness is a punishment for sins. Initially, I felt that this interpretation of illness was due to faulty religious education prior to the onset of illness. Now it appears to me that these patients reflect a universal human tendency to avoid the anxiety of feeling helpless in the hands of what seems to be an impersonal, irrational fate. Affirming that I am ill with cancer because God is punishing me for my sins is a more tolerable, ego-satisfying interpretation than concluding that I am victim of a disease process which is indifferent to my personal identity.[6]

By interpreting the tragic as a consequence of our sins or even of carelessness, we are reassured that we exist as individuals of significance. Any meaning given to a situation is better than a situation which is not only tragic, but is also without predetermined meaning. It may seem we are not being dealt with fairly in accordance with our merits, but at least we are not ignored. We matter to Someone. If God is punishing us, we have tangible evidence God is aware of us and has taken special notice of us.

I remember a counselee in our Clinical Pastoral Education Program who called himself a "living Murphy's Law." If it could happen to him, it did. I was surprised one day to hear him say to the intern chaplain, "Well, at least I know I am a Christian. God still cares about me."

"How is that?" was the response to his comment.

"Well, last week a pastor told me that God sends us problems to punish us and make us get back to him. If we are his children, he punishes us. When things go wrong, at least I know God still loves me."

His childhood experiences in a dysfunctional family taught him to interpret abuse as evidence of love. He continued to make poor choices which resulted in problems. He resisted doing the work that could change those patterns. He found a strange comfort in seeing his problems as an assurance that he was important to God!

Even the plight of Job, if understood in this light, would seem tolerable. However, we shall discover in chapter six that Job refused to interpret his tragedies in this light. Job was not willing to accept his suffering as a just reward for his wrongs nor as proof that God loved him. Job would not accept this even at the risk of discovering that no one, not even God, cared about his suffering.

"What did I do that was so bad I deserved to be raped? I was only eight years old," Thomas would ask.
"I was only three!" Aaron Kushner might add. *"What did I do to deserve to die of a rare disease?"*

As Susan suggested, blaming the victim is a way we try to reassure ourselves that the world is not as bad as we secretly fear. In an effort to quiet our fears, we offer hollow assurances by blaming those who suffer.

The Green River Task Force is a well-known investigative team in Washington and Oregon. Created in the early eighties, it investigated a series of forty-eight murders during the period of 1982 to 1984. A person known as "The Green River Killer" murdered forty-eight young women.[7] The massive effort to solve the killings began July

15, 1982, when the body of Wendy Lee Coffield, 16, was found near the Green River in Tacoma, Washington. All of the victims were young runaways, prostitutes, and topless dancers. The sheer number of these crimes magnified their hideousness. Forty-eight murders—the nation's worst unsolved serial murder case.

By July 5, 1987, the Task Force had spent over nine million dollars on efforts that included a computer programmed with over eighteen thousand suspect "tip sheets" in an unsuccessful search for the serial killer. The sudden cessation of the murders in 1984 seems to indicate that the murderer moved on to another part of the nation. In December 1988, the Task Force made a nationwide appeal to the public to help solve the murders through the production of a documentary movie, *Manhunt: A Chance to End a Nightmare*. It was aired on national prime-time TV.

Examples of the subtle efforts we use to deceive ourselves into feeling safe in the face of such horror were heard in the comments from people "on the street."

"What do you expect? When you do those kinds of things (prostitution, run away from home), *you can expect to get into trouble."*

"If the blacks had stayed in their place, James Earl Ray would not have been pressured to kill Martin Luther King."

"If the Jews hadn't been so greedy, Hitler wouldn't have driven them to slaughter."

"If people would just work, they would not be poor."

"If girls would just say 'no,' boys would not take advantage of them."

No matter how naive the effort, blaming the victim seems to offer an acceptable but shallow sense of meaning to suffering and evil. In my work, I have observed this process repeatedly. Some patients have an incredible determination to interpret cancer, car accidents, AIDS, and an endless variety of life-threatening events as God's punishment for their sin.

Corazon Amuroa talked lightly with her roommates as they exchanged bits of news about the day. They shared experiences from contact with patients at the hospital. They exchanged class notes and shared concerns about the next exam. It was hot in Chicago that night, July 13, 1966. The South Chicago Community Hospital where Corazon had worked that day was a few blocks away. It felt good to be away from the pain and sickness she faced there. The student nurses' dormitory was quiet; lights were out. Corazon and her eight roommates were in bed. No one knows where he came from, but "he" was suddenly there, armed with a knife and a pistol. First he bound and gagged each of nine student nurses with strips of cloth torn from a sheet. Then he led them, one at a time, to another room and one by one Richard Speck stabbed them to death.

Corazon escaped the slaughter by rolling under a bunk bed and hiding while Speck was out of the room killing her friends. Corazon and her roommates prayed. Eight young women pleaded for help as they were stabbed to death.

> And David cried, *"Oh Lord, fight for me.... Lord, how long will you stand there doing nothing?"*

Corazon Amuroa survived. In the darkness and confusion, Speck did not see her hiding under the bed. She lived to identify him a few weeks later. A tattoo on his arm gave him away. It read "Born to raise hell!"[8]

Millions of innocent victims who have suffered and died at the hands of evil have asked the same question Thomas asked. Many of these victims were guilty only of being where a Richard Speck chose to do evil. Some are quick to note that Corazon was spared. No doubt she and her family were grateful and thanked God for sparing her. But there's the inevitable question: Did God spare Corazon Amuroa? Did God miraculously intervene in her behalf? Did God intervene for her but not for her eight roommates? If so, why? Why Corazon? Why not one of the others? Why not all of the others?

> *"How long will you stand there doing nothing?"* David asks.
> *"Where was God when I was raped?"* Thomas asks.
> *"Why did God make me suffer and die?"* asks Aaron.
> *"Why didn't God take better care of me?* asks a five-year-old child near death.

It was a warm sunny day in Beaverton, Oregon, June 20, 1988—the first day of summer vacation. Donna Shonkwiler was driving south on Menlo Drive that midmorning; the traffic was normal. No one knows for sure what happened. Suddenly the green Volkswagen veered to the right. The sound of screeching brakes pierced the air, echoing throughout the apartment neighborhood. Donna struggled to regain control of her car as it struck a pedestrian crossing sign. The careening vehicle crashed through bushes, crossed an intersection, and continued down the sidewalk on the west side of the street. The sounds of crashing metal and breaking glass penetrated the air as the small car finally came to a halt, wrapping around a utility pole. Donna, critically injured, was trapped in the wreckage. The paramedics removed the top of the car to extricate her from the tangled metal.

The lurching car left a path strewn with debris, skid marks, and the bodies of three young boys: Carlos Rojano, eight years old, with his brother, Marcos, six, and their friend, Juan Olivares, seven. They were enroute to a neighborhood park and had been walking on the sidewalk on the west side of Menlo Drive.

Carlos was killed on impact; Marcos died later that night. Juan survived with head wounds and multiple trauma. Only weeks earlier the Rojano family had moved from California to distance their kids from the dangers of street gangs and drugs. They had given up their home and work to provide their children with a safer place to grow up.

One witness to the accident said, "Kids walk down that sidewalk every day. Thank God, my kid was in the house."[9]

"Thank God!" Could a father say anything less? But what do we mean when we say, "Thank God mine was spared"? If God spared the child of the eyewitness by keeping him in the house, where was God and what was God doing when Carlos and Marcos were run down and killed?

Does God alter the laws of nature and circumstances and spare people? I have always been uncomfortable with spotlight testimonials about God's miraculous intervention that spared someone from a tragic or horrible situation. Some say God did a miraculous thing and saved Corazon. But what about the other eight? They surely pleaded and prayed for mercy to live. Why were Carlos and Marcos killed but not Juan? Did God intervene?

I know many situations where it seems miraculous interventions occurred. There are times when situations change and physical conditions are altered without any apparent logical explanation. Sometimes these things happen when people prayed; other times they happen without a word of prayer. That such events occur is not the question. What we need is a fuller understanding about how these events are related to God. Where is God at these times?

When I hear someone say, "God spared me," I feel uneasy. A newscaster on national television was interviewing a man who was the only survivor of a commuter plane crash. He said, "It was a miracle. God spared me!" To survive a plane crash is indeed miraculous, but what did the survivor mean? If what he claims is true and God did break into the natural order of predictable events and effected the circumstances of that plane crash to keep that particular man from dying, what does that force us to believe? If the survivor's claim is true, we must conclude that God spared him, but killed the other twenty-nine passengers on the plane! If God spares some, then those who perish are, at best, victims of God's refusal to intervene on their behalf.

In the closing scenes of the poignant film, *The Mission,* the papal representative has finished reading the report of the savage elimination of the mountain Indian village and Jesuit mission, San Carlos. The Jesuit mission and the village were obstacles to the political and economic exploitations of the Portuguese and the Spanish governments. The papal representative was to resolve a dispute concerning control of the territory where the village and mission were located. The village and its mission, removed from the protection of the Church, were left to the mercy of the Portuguese and Spanish settlers. The papal representative reads the report of the assault on the village and it stuns him. The entire village and mission had been ruthlessly destroyed. The priest and most of the villagers were killed. His Eminence returns to the Spanish representative who led the assault.

"And you have the effrontery to tell me this slaughter was necessary?"

"I did what I had to do," he responds, "given the legitimate purpose which you sanctioned. I would have to say, yes. In truth, yes."

The papal representative sits in silence.

Señor Hunter, the Portuguese representative speaks. "You had no alternative, your Eminence. We must work in the world. The world is thus."

"No, Señor Hunter," the papal representative replies, as he moves to an open window. "Thus have we made the world."

His face is doleful with the realization of the carnage. Staring out the window, he adds quietly, "Thus have I made it."

Thomas asked, *"Where was God when I was raped?"*

Thomas did not miraculously survive a plane crash. He did not escape from a homicidal maniac. He was a young boy who was raped! Raped, not because he chose a perverted life-style. Raped, not because at the age of eight he was so committed to evil that he needed some drastic form of divinely authorized punishment to bring him to his senses. Raped, not because the horror of such an experience was designed to make him a better person. Raped, not because God wanted him to know he could stand it. Raped, not because he was a pawn God and Satan had chosen as a gambit in some cosmic chess game between them. Raped, but not because God willfully caused it or because God willingly gave permission for it!

The evil choice of his father was the one reason, the only reason Thomas's father raped him. We can call his father's actions "homopedophilia compulsions," "sick behavior," or just plain "evil." What we call it is important, but it is not the most important.

What we call the father's behavior is merely an effort to explain it. At best, it is only a descriptive reason for what he did. The issue is still the same. Why was Thomas raped? He was raped because his father chose to rape him. It was not Thomas nor God; it was Thomas's father who made it thus!

Still the question hangs unanswered: *Where* was God when Thomas was raped?

If God was not sitting on a divine throne passively watching or standing at the foot of a bed waiting to come and comfort him, where was God? What was the Almighty doing?

Could it be that God was preoccupied with universal matters, too distracted by the workings of the planets to be concerned with one individual event, even the raping of a little boy?

NOTES

1. "Temptation" is a translation of *peirasmos*, "to entice one to do wrong." Thayer's *Greek-English Lexicon of the New Testament* (Nashville, Tennessee: Broadman, 1978), p. 409.

2. *Ibid.,* p. 498.

3. Archibald MacLeish, *J.B.* (Boston: Houghton Mifflin Company, 1956), pp. 48, 50.

4. Harold S. Kushner, *When Bad Things Happen to Good People* (New

York: Schocken Books, 1981), p. 29.

5. M. Scott Peck, *People of the Lie* (New York: Simon and Schuster, 1983), p. 62.

6. Edward E. Thornton, *Theology and Pastoral Counseling* (Englewood Cliffs, New Jersey: Prentice Hall, Inc., 1964), p. 35.

7. *The Oregonian,* Sunday, July 5, 1987.

8. *Chicago Sun-Times,* August 23, 1987.

9. *The Oregonian,* Tuesday, June 21, 1988.

CHAPTER THREE

THE ANSWERS:
"God Was Carrying Me";
"God Was In Me"

I glanced at my watch again—3:40 p.m; twenty minutes left in the session. My thoughts came as slowly as time passed. I loosened my tie some more. For a moment my thoughts were on the chaplain interns observing the session from behind the mirrored window. I felt tinges of embarrassment. There is nothing like being on the spot in front of one's students. Thomas interrupted my thoughts.

"You know, Chaplain, I remember a story someone once told...." He paused as if listening. Everyone waited to hear the story.

"What story?" someone asked.

Thomas began. *"It was about this man who had this dream. He dreamed he was walking along with God. As they walked along, he began to look back on his life, like he could see everywhere he had gone. As he looked back, he could see footprints in the sand. And he realized that they were his footprints and God's. But then he saw that there were some places where there was only one set of footprints. As he thought about it, he realized that the places where there was only one set of footprints were the hardest times in his life. There was only one set of footprints in every place he had had trouble or pain or felt hopeless. Well, this made him mad, because he thought God had left him every time he needed any help. So he turned to God and asked him about it. He said, 'Lord, every time I came to a hard place there was only one set of footprints. Why did you leave me at the times I needed you the most?'"* Thomas paused.

"*And God said to him, 'I didn't ever leave you. There is only one set of footprints during the bad times because I was CAR-RYING you.*" Thomas paused again. He seemed to be weighing his own words.

"*Carrying me...God was carrying me while I was being raped? No way! If God was carrying me when I was raped then I am...mad! I didn't ask him to carry me. I asked him to stop it!*"

Thomas startled everyone with the sudden burst of anger at his own words. Again the room became silent. There was no silence in my head. My mind was a jumble of thoughts mixing and meshing with feelings. Thomas had loosed some questions and thoughts I had long confined to the back corners of my mind. The group was uneasy. Some were uncomfortable with Thomas's anger. The story confused others. I could appreciate their confusion. I don't like that story called "Footprints." It is quite popular and is often mounted on plaques in gift shops. It also appears on greeting cards designed to encourage. As Thomas talked, I understood why that story bothers me.

As is often the case, good sentiment holds a place in many religious songs and stories, but they are based on bad ideas about God that are not true. At first glance, this story is comforting and assures us that God takes care of us when we are at our worst, even though we may not be aware of it. But can we really believe that the story about God is true?

The concept of God's behaving like a good parent carrying a tired or weary child is beautiful. For some, this conjures up memories from their childhood when their father or mother carried them home after a tiring day in the park. This was not Thomas's childhood memory. If what the story says about God is correct, then we are left with an inexplicable situation; we have to accept something about God that is inconceivable. Thomas saw the inevitable conclusion. If God carried him during those bad times—when bad things happened to him—then God also carried him while he was being raped! Was God holding an innocent child in Divine arms while he was raped? Was God holding Juan and Carlos when Donna killed them with her car? Is that the reason they failed to jump out of the way—God was holding them?

His experience of the absence of God confused Thomas. Where

was God when he was raped? For years his feelings about God had vacillated. At times, anger and an outright rejection of God overcame him. At other times he made a sincere effort to worship God and to trust God to help him overcome his mental problems. At the moment, Thomas seemed to be less troubled by the uncertainty of where God was when he was raped than the idea of God's carrying him while he was being raped.

David was perplexed at the thought of God's standing by and doing nothing while he was falsely accused. Thomas was horrified at the thought of God's holding him while he was raped.

As Thomas responded to the story, the sweat on my back turned to ice and a sudden chill enveloped me. The image of God—the Divine Father—holding a young child while he was raped was inconceivable, even repulsive. This must have been furthermost from the mind of the author. What do we mean when we assure ourselves that God is with us in our times of need?

An encouraging verse is found in Hebrews 13:5. "For he (God) has said, 'I will never leave you nor forsake you.' " The historical context of this inspired verse intensifies its poetic encouragement. It is the closing scene in Moses' career as the leader of Israel. Moses is turning the leadership of Israel over to Joshua. In his words of farewell to Joshua, Moses assures him that God will be with him. Moses says:

> *"Be strong and of good courage, do not fear or be in dread...for it is the Lord your God who goes with you; he will not fail you or forsake you"* (Dt 31:6).

The historical setting of this verse was emotionally charged with memories of God's faithfulness to Israel. Against this backdrop the writer assures his readers that they can count on God to be there when they need him. Several Scripture verses like this one are based on the theological concept that God is present with us in life. One finds homiletical support for this belief in the writer's use of consecutive negatives in his sentence structure.[1] It reads as a carefully crafted statement, constructed in a manner that has the fullest impact possible on the reader. The statement is a compound negative which could read, "I will *never, no not ever, no never* leave you."

From this and similar passages we conclude that God, involved in human experience, is with us at all times, even when we suffer and die. I have often found encouragement and help in this belief, comfort and strength in this awareness. But I have grave misgivings in the context of unprovoked ravishing of the innocent. How is God with me in moments like that?

Thomas needed more than a God who was nearby, waiting to comfort him as soon as "it" was over. He needed more than a distant God who knew what was happening and understood vicariously what Thomas was going through.

Thomas's words frightened me. I didn't know where God was when Thomas was raped. But I knew for certain that the story was not the answer. God was not carrying Thomas or Aaron or Beth or Karen or Juan or Carlos when they suffered unjustly or died without a reason.

I have worked in medical centers for more than eighteen years. My experience there has forced me to come to terms with some hard facts. For each account of a miraculous intervention/healing that spares the innocent child or helpless elderly person or dying patient, a hundred others are not spared. They die. Was God punishing these people? Were they people who needed to be taught a lesson? Were they people God had forgotten, who didn't believe in God, who didn't pray? I think not.

Many of them were, in fact, people of great faith who prayed earnestly and lived good, clean, and loving lives. Yet their faith and prayers and the prayers of others were to no avail. Nothing happened to change the circumstances. No miracle occurred. God did not intervene to save them. Their worlds fell apart, they lost, they hurt, they suffered, they died. And where was God? As a chaplain, I stood by their beds, sat with them and talked with them and their loved ones. I tried to give them support, comfort, and encouragement. I assured them that God does care, God is concerned about them, God is with them. Some believed, some did not. The most difficult times were those when nothing changed, not even the silence, the silence that defies faith and calls forth faith.

In those moments I continued to believe God was there, but that belief, at times, was very vague. What does it mean to believe God is there when all you have is a waning feeling, a wavering trust that somehow God is present? Even the feeling is evasive; sometimes it is just not there. It is hard to trust at those moments, even though you continue doing and saying the "right" things. Is God's presence dependent on feelings? Like Thomas, I really wanted to know where

God is when I'm not comforted or helped. When an internal decision to believe is all I have, how is God present?

Traditional theologians and philosophers claim that God is everywhere at all times. But does that mean God is, in reality, nowhere at any time? My belief in God's presence has on some occasions been little more than a small knot tied at the end of a threadbare rope. It may shock some people to hear such words from a minister. These words may not be spoken often but they are often in the thoughts of ministers and non-ministers alike. Because we are afraid to be honest about our questions and our faith, others assume we have no fears or doubts. Unfortunately, they judge themselves harshly on the assumption that our silence means we do not share their concerns.

I am convinced that God was involved with every person and event noted earlier. When bad things happen, God is there. People were spared; others were not spared. People got well. People died. People escaped suffering and tragedy. People suffered and tragedy devastated them. In it all, God was there. But how?

What happened next within the group in the next few minutes is not clear. I remember the prolonged silence. Momentarily, I considered ending the group session with some clinical cliché like, "Well, that gives us all something to think about." Then someone said something. I don't remember who spoke or what they said. I was simply not there.

Thoughts of a long-forgotten time and place surfaced in my mind. It was all so clear, much like watching a rerun of an old movie—one you have seen so many times that you think you know every part of each scene. But you don't. There is always that insignificant sequence you've forgotten. Upon recall, it is that brief forgotten scene which holds a special meaning.

I had not forgotten Sarah. She was one of my first long-term pastoral counselees who taught me some valuable lessons about counseling. For three and a half years Sarah struggled with major life issues that had a tremendous effect on her. I would never forget her.

When I met her, Sarah thought she was forty-one. She wasn't sure since the partial records from the orphanage where she spent her childhood were contradictory. The orphanage had closed long ago and the records were housed in a small college in another state. Sarah traveled there during our work to do personal research on her history. A discrepancy in the entries stated her age in 1941 as eight. Two years later the same records noted her age as six. Was she forty-one or forty-three? Her appearance denied both; she looked thirty. She had the classic natural beauty of a native North American, petite and just under five feet tall. Her long dark hair nearly equaled her height. Sarah, a bright and intelligent woman, lived with her preschool daughter and used her secretarial and managerial skills to provide for the two of them.

Sarah, gifted with words, made her journals read like a novel. She often wrote to God with the salutation, "Dear Ubba."[2] Her relationship with God was personal and real. Although she lacked formal training in theology, her understanding of God was amazing. She spoke with and about God with such simplicity and beauty that it was at times mystifying. Sarah's relationship with God developed out of her experiences. She had a rough life and there were times when she was angry. She would rail against the unresponsive universe and ask, "Where is God?"

Her problem centered on confusion about her sexual identity and unresolved rage stemming from childhood abuse. Sarah was not fond of organized religion. I still marvel that we worked through her hostility toward men and representatives of religion, symbolized in me as a chaplain at a medical center that Catholic sisters operated.

Suddenly Sarah's image focused in my mind. I could see her clearly, sitting in the large chair in my former office. I was struck by her size—tiny and childlike. Sitting in that chair, her head was barely visible over the tops of the high-cushioned arms.

"Chaplain Horace O. Duke," I heard her say.

The tone of her voice quickened my inner thoughts. Sarah addressed me in that formal manner only when she was angry or intensely focused on getting my full attention. She did not sound angry.

It was strange. For a moment I felt I had literally left the group room. I was two floors above in the office I used ten years earlier. In the memory recall, I watched her closely as she spoke again.

"Don't you remember?" she asked. Her voice was soft on the "ears" of my mind.

I remembered the anguish Sarah relived as she talked about the sexual abuse she endured as an adolescent. Once a week one of the orphanage staff took Sarah to her room for special instructions about sex. Sarah remembered the room. It was small and plainly furnished. She remembered the bed, the pewter water pitcher and basin that sat on the small table. She remembered the crucifix on the wall at the foot of the bed. On the bed at the foot of the crucifix, an attendant raped Sarah with the smooth curved end of a fireplace poker. The painful ritual occurred each week. She went through the degrading ordeal under the watchful eyes of the crucifix hanging on the wall. Each week Sarah would steel herself for the pain. She would not cry aloud. She would shed no tears. But in her mind she cried, she prayed, she pleaded for help from the "God on the cross." Each week she suffered. Each week the "God on the cross" did nothing but hang there and watch.

As a child, Sarah knew where God was when she was raped. It offered her some comfort to think that while she was being raped God was "on a cross." That kind of God at least knew something about what it is like to suffer, to be raped! Many years later she began to understand where God had been when she was raped. Again, I heard Sarah's voice.

"I know..." She paused. *"I know where God was during those times I was raped. He wasn't on that cross. God was IN me. I mean really, like He was me, a little girl being raped. I mean like God was me! When I was being raped, God had come down off that cross and was in me. That is where God was. He was a little girl being raped, being raped with me. God was within me all that time and I didn't even know it."*

I felt like I had just awakened from a deep, sound sleep. I was "back" in the group. No one seemed to notice that I had been "away." Time was no longer a concern. I felt calm for the first time since the group started.

"Thomas," I began, *"I think I know where God was when you were raped."*

I could hear my voice clearly. It was soft and the tone reflected the inner sense of awe I was experiencing. My words sounded well chosen. They were. They were more a quote than a statement.

"Thomas, you are right. God was not carrying you when you

were raped. Thomas, God was in you. God was in you when you were raped. God was a little boy: you. God felt it all with you—the helpless, painful hell of being raped. Thomas, God was in you when you were raped."

Once again the group was silent. Thomas spoke.

"In me? God abused with me? I've never heard that before," Thomas pondered aloud.
"God in me...God, a little boy raped within me? I'll have to think about that."

The hour had flown by. There were the normal silent looks and a few "thank you's" as the group left the room. Those who spoke did so in hushed tones. Thomas and I left the room without a word; each of us was deep in his own thoughts.

It was silent again....

It was a silence of a different kind.

NOTES

1. *The Pulpit Commentary,* Vol. 21, p. 399.
2. "Ubba" is said to be Eskimo for "grandfather," the gentle, loving trusted one. To Sarah, the term symbolized the central characteristics represented in the New Testament term, "Abba Father." *Abba* is an Aramaic word found only three times in the New Testament. It approximates a personal name in contrast to "father," with which it is always joined in the New Testament. Greek-speaking Jews added the Greek word "pater" (father) from the language they used. Abba, framed by the lips of infants, betokens unreasoning trust. "Father" expresses an intelligent appreciation of the relationship. The amplified meaning of "Abba Father" is expressed well in Sarah's expression "Ubba"—"grandfather." W. E. Vine, *An Expository Dictionary of Old and New Testament Words* (Old Tappan, New Jersey: Fleming H. Revell Company, 1981), p. 9.

CHAPTER FOUR

THE MYSTERY:
God, Power, and Powerlessness

The silence continued. I sat motionless as I studied Karen closely for hints of reaction. She did not speak. I could see the predictable and subtle changes in her face. Blotches on her forehead and neck signaled the intensity of all that was going on inside her. Every therapeutic intervention is a calculated risk. Karen knew I had worked with other persons who survived the trauma of incest. Our work was going well and I was confident in the level of trust we had developed over the past year.

How would Karen react to Sarah's answer to Thomas's question? I knew Karen would never get over her incestuous injuries. There are some things in life one does not get over. But Karen would recover. She would feel clean and whole and, in time, would adjust to the loss of her childhood and enjoy a healthy adult life. The dominating negative themes would be altered. Should she choose otherwise—that, too, was an option—I would have to live with her choice.

My concern over the intervention disappeared. It was timely.

In the words of Robert Frost's popular poem,[1] Karen still had many "miles to go" and "promises to keep" before the consequences of her childhood ordeal could finally be put to rest. Karen's promises were internal commitments she made to herself as a child. They were based on negative beliefs she held about herself, deep wounds covered with emotional and spiritual scars. At times, Karen's affective experience was severely deadened. She handled intimate interactions much like a person who tries to feel pure silk with calloused fingertips. Karen's underlying themes of self-condemnation, guilt, and anger set her up to become entangled in unhealthy relationships similar to those she learned in her sick and highly dysfunctional family.

There are many other facets to Karen. She is a delightful, energetic, intelligent person. She worked with professional people and managed her professional life in a mature but, at times, compulsive manner. Her job called for a great deal of coordination and management skills. In addition, she maintained a four-point grade average in a local university.

As I stated in chapter two, Karen's experience, though similar to Beth's, was much worse. Karen's story is incredible. How could anyone withstand so much abuse? I didn't doubt Karen's story, but how could such extremes actually happen—and for so many years?

Karen seemed to sense my initial reaction. Other therapists likely had the same difficulty. Early in our work she voluntarily brought documents verifying her story to a session. These included reports from Children's Service Division and the court order removing her from her home and placing her in foster care. Her wounds were too deep and her pain too real to doubt; it did happen.

Her earliest images of abuse began about age three. Her father and her uncle fondled her. By age five, one—maybe both—had penetrated her. From early childhood into her teens, her older brothers routinely had sex with her. On some occasions, they forced her to have sex with their friends. From her earliest memory, sex in one form or another was a part of family life. She learned to survive in that environment. When she recalled some of the ways she had adapted, she felt confusion and guilt. This was an ongoing battle in our work: to stop judging the child for the sins of her abusers.

Once again I was lost in silence.

My mind wandered for a moment. I recalled how often anger toward the abused child is a common theme in the thoughts of the adult survivor of sexual abuse. I could hear Karen's oft-repeated question:

> *"If she* (speaking of herself as a child) *was so smart at finding ways to survive, why didn't she figure out a way to stop it?"*

I never cease to be amazed at the anger and judgment adult survivors of sexual abuse feel toward themselves as children. Karen was a living example of Scott Peck's "law of child development."

When a child is grossly confronted by significant evil in its parents,

58

it will most likely misinterpret the situation and believe that the evil resides in itself.[2]

Karen "misinterpreted" the "significant evil" which had "grossly confronted" her as a child. She, as Peck predicts, believed that the evil she endured "resided in her." This incredible trait is native to victims of childhood sexual abuse.

Once again I recalled all that Sarah had taught me. Victims of incest—like victims of most kinds of abuse—are prone to blame themselves. But victims of incest have an added difficulty. They are afraid no one will believe them. Sarah spoke of this years before in one of her early journal prayers. The entry followed conversations with her sister, Leah. Leah, too, had been abused in the orphanage. Sarah wrote:

> ...Leah and I have talked and talked.... I don't know if it is helping.... It hurts more sometimes—too much hurting! Leah was hurt too, sadistically so. Leah says she never discussed it with anyone. Unless someone experienced what we did, it would be too hard to believe. Horace, thank you! Thank you for believing!

I had many questions when I listened initially to Karen's story. How could so much bad happen to one person for so many years and someone not do something about it? How? My God, how? Matthew, a brother, told her he sometimes felt bad about it. "But what could I do? I couldn't stop the others." That, above all else, seemed to haunt Karen. No one—not mother, father, brothers, not even Matthew nor the school teacher she confided in tried to stop it. No one did anything! Not even God. Karen carried a residue of doubt about so many things. She needed the security of having someone really believe her. For Karen, this security was an indispensable part of her accepting the truth about what happened. Out of this could come an appropriate redirecting of the anger and rage that she held bottled up within herself.

Karen's eyes darted from side to side. I contained my renewed discomfort. What was she feeling? What was she thinking? How would she react to Sarah's claim that "God was in her"?

I did not expect her response to be positive at that point. This was not the first time we talked about her confusion. Where was God in all of this? I was prepared to deal with her affinity for twisting any potential positive into a certain negative.

I waited. Her eyes became fixed as she looked squarely into mine.

"What does that mean? God was in him?"

Her voice was flat and cautious. The tone hinted at anger. I could hear the hesitancy behind a slight indication of curiosity. It was as if she had an unformulated premonition of where that concept might lead her. She waited for my response. My anxiety rose.

That was a sensitive, powerful area. I was careful not to get caught up in word games about religion. Karen was an expert at word games. I could not afford to play word games with myself. I was beginning to realize that the urgency I felt about Karen's view of God was partly my own need to re-examine who God is to me. I did not believe God sends or allows the kind of evil that people like Karen experience. However, I had never been forced to ferret out all of that for myself. I have had some bad experiences and most of them—not all—were the results of my own foolish or bad choices— my sins. No one has ever done anything horribly evil to me. I had faced the death of a daughter, the death of a father, a divorce, dis-appointments, and failures. But I had not faced raw dehumanizing evil.

When one is fifty years old, the thought of being dead at fifty-three is devastating. Nancy and I had become increasingly concerned about the difficulties I was having with my left arm. At first the changes were so subtle it was hard to believe. It was the fall of 1984. I was stacking firewood when I realized I couldn't pick up a small piece of split firewood with my left hand! The first six months of 1985 were filled with endless tests, even exploratory surgery—each with the same result—no diagnosis. The weakness grew and I lost more control of my left arm and hand. It was November 1985, two weeks before Thanksgiving. Nancy and I were returning from the University of California Medical School where we had gone for a neurological consultation. The diagnosis confirmed our worst fears. I had ALS (amyotrophic lateral sclerosis) commonly known as Lou Gehrig's disease. The silence was deafening as we drove home from San Francisco. Introverts that we are, Nancy and I did not talk of our inner sadness and fear.

As the doctor and I discussed my accelerated deterioration, I pressed the question of prognosis: "What are we up against, given what is known about ALS? What are we facing? What is the best guess?"

"Well...." There was a long pause. "Considering the rapid deterioration you are experiencing, we can expect...a wheelchair. My best guess would be two years."

"Two years?" I responded. "Two years until I'm in a wheelchair or...two years until I'm dead?"

"Dead."

There was no pain, no physical discomfort. It was strange. "I have a crippling disease that will kill me and yet I feel well." What I had talked about with many people was happening to me. I was dying.

Since 1973 I had taught college courses on death and dying. I conducted workshops on the ways to deal with the issues of death and dying. Every lecture I gave and each paper I wrote began with the same point: "The number one issue in death and dying is one's own death. The first issue professionals face in working with terminal patients is one's own death." I believed that. I thought about it and talked of my own death many times. I tried to see life through the reality of death, my death. Trying to live with the concept that death is a natural part of living had enriched the meaning and experiences of my life in many ways. I had discovered that life looks different when seen through the prism of the reality of death. The difference is good. Death can be understood as a reluctant friend who reminds one of the importance of living life to the fullest. In this way, death becomes a point of reference for assessing the value one gives to his or her life.

My view of death and life grew out of my faith and a special relationship I had with Rea Thrash. I met Rea during my first pastorate in a small Texas community in the late 1950s. Rea, an interesting man in his forties, had a serious heart problem. A pacemaker stimulated his heart to maintain a proper rhythm. At that time I had only a limited understanding of Rea's situation. I thought of a pacemaker as some kind of flashlight battery sewn into his chest. Rea and I had many conversations about life and death. With the urgings of his wife, I encouraged Rea to take things easier. On several occasions, I tried to talk him out of going fishing alone. He loved to fish and occasionally went out alone in his boat. I frequently asked him, "Rea, what would you do if you were fishing alone and that thing stopped working?" His answer, heavy with a Texas accent, was always the same: "Preacher, like I've told you, I would die." He would pause, then add, "But a man's not ready to live until he's ready to die."

Rea was a devout Christian, but because of discomfort in crowds Rea did not attend church services. However, on the day we brought Rea to church for his funeral I had a keen sense of peace as I spoke of him to those gathered to mourn his death. I concluded the service with these words: "Rea did not live a long life, but if ever a man lived life, he did. He was a man who lived, ready to die."

I taught that to others and I believed it myself until I had only two years to live. As the shock wore off and the reality of the prognosis settled in our minds, the first question that came to Nancy and me was not the predictable, "Why? Why me?" The question we asked was "Why not? Why not me?" It happens to other people and sooner or later it happens to all. Why should it not happen to us? We didn't like it and we'd change it if we could. If we could not, we would continue to do exactly as we had been doing all along. We would keep on living until....

Where was God in all of this? Did I pray? Did I ask for healing or expect a miracle? Many friends did; they urged me to seek divine intervention. My pastor was confused that I did not accept the offer of a special prayer service. At one time that would have been my first reaction. During those first months I talked with God about my situation. I expressed disappointment and sadness, my fear, my sense of utter powerlessness and the consequent anger. God knew I was not ready to die, yet those prayer conversations always ended the same way. Every time I thought about having ALS or talked with friends about it, somewhere from within I found myself saying, "It is not fair. I don't want to die. Still—it happens to others. Why not me?" I could not get away from it. I accept without question the good life, so why not the bad? Why not me?

I didn't need answers. Rather, I needed to ask the right questions. Moché the Beadle was right again. Eli Wiesel once asked Moché why he prayed. Moché replied, "I pray to the God within me that He will give me the strength to ask Him the right questions.... [God's answers] come from the depths of the soul, and they stay there until death. You will find the true answers...only within yourself!"[3]

I did not pray to be healed. I was aware, though, that many did pray for me to be healed, and I appreciated their efforts. Their concern and their faith were affirming. I prayed for God to be with me as I lived with all that was happening. I wasn't really ready to die, but I had no choice about that. Does one ever have a choice about dying? Much of the time I was calm about the diagnosis. At other private times the sadness was overpowering and I raged with anger at my impotence in the face of my impending death. But I had an underlying belief that God was with me. God was tolerant of—and a part of—my cries and my rage. What I felt was powerful. What I believed proved to be even more powerful.

I know God was with me at that time, but it is difficult to express. There were no special messages, no visions, no insights. Now I see that God was in me, experiencing my fear and sadness, my struggles to cope with the realization that everything I found meaningful in life was coming to an unexpected, untimely end. I was powerless to stop it. I would always be powerless to stop it. God, too, was powerless to stop my death, powerless to intervene in what was happening to me. I believed God had done something about the consequences of death. I believed in life after death. But there is a time and a place for death and God cannot stop it. The ratio has remained constant from the beginning—one out of every birth ends in death. I began to see that God did understand. What happened in life did not determine my relationship with God. My choice determined this. My response to all that happens to me in life determines the kind of relationship I have with God. As Ella Wheeler Wilcox wrote:

> One ship drives east and another drives west,
> With the selfsame winds that blow.
> 'Tis the set of sails and not the gales,
> Which tells us the way to go.

There are no certainties to the winds of life. That was Job's shattering discovery. You plant your fields and birth your children. You make choices, do your best and sometimes less than your best. Faith in God and living a good life have never guaranteed protection from loss, disappointment, or death. However, many among us have never stopped trying to get God to function that way. Faith in God guarantees only one thing: the awareness that God is within us in all things. No, God could not stop my disease or death, but God could be and was, indeed, with me in it. Within that awareness resides the potential for all that is called miraculous.

I began to see that God and I are bound by the same rules of human experience. God and I were together in this thing called life and death. God would not heal me because I was God's favorite person or the lucky beneficiary of a choice move in some divine-satanic chess game. Nor would I suffer and die because I was on God's "hit list." All that was happening to me was a part of the risk of living, of being human. God does not give disease to some, allow it for others, prevent and cure it for still others. Neurological diseases are a part of this world just as is famine and baldness. God does not decide who will be bald, who will be blind, who will have ALS, who will die now and who will live only to die later. Contrary to some popular and traditional religious ideas, such things are not within God's control. The reality of God's creation—God's choice to be a part of the creative process—precluded that as being possible.

The creative capacity of God brought the universe and all within it into existence. God was the source and is the dynamic means that gives it life and continued existence. Within the created order, God set into motion the processes for being human. These processes and how they affect the world were, and remain, in divine control. God named the created world to come into being; it is still becoming. The Genesis story reflects this inspired meaning. "In the beginning God created the heavens and the earth….The earth was without form and void, and darkness was upon the face of the deep and the Spirit of God was moving over the face of the waters…" (Gn 1:1-2). God set creation into motion and entered into its becoming. But in doing so, God relinquished to humanity and to the on-going creative process of nature the power to control what it will become. Thus, we have made the world of humankind whatever it is throughout the eons of time.

It is clear to me now. God was doing something during those years when death seemed imminent. But God was not doing what some people thought. Each day I lived with the physical limitations, the powerful emotional and spiritual dynamics of my impending death. I had no difficulty doing my work as chaplain and counselor. Now and then I was stunned when I realized that had I been a surgeon, or a mechanic, or a ditch digger, I would already be disabled. But I was still able to do things that expressed the meaning of my life. I knew I was doing the only thing I could do with an awareness that God was doing the only thing God could do: entering with me into my experience. God could not stop what was happening to me any more than I could. God could not run away from it any more than I could. God was, as Sarah might put it, a fifty-year-old man facing what it means to encounter disability, uncertainty, and death.

Nancy and I began to prepare for my approaching disability and eventual death. We looked at our lives, at who we were, and what we were doing. There was little we wanted to change. We became less involved in some activities and created new space and time for the two of us. We spent more days at the Oregon seaside and on the trout streams of Oregon and Montana.

We lived and waited, expecting the worst. But it didn't happen. Two years later I returned to the doctor for a checkup. His examination validated what I had been feeling. I had regained strength in the nerves and muscles of my left arm. According to medical science, this does not happen with ALS patients. The doctor withdrew the diagnosis. Today the use of my left arm and hand is only slightly compromised. I type these words with both hands, although I tend to use a modified hunt and peck system with my left hand. My condition, however, remains undiagnosed.

The Rev. Pete Zagel, a chaplain in the alcohol treatment program at Providence Medical Center in Portland, had an office near mine. In the summer of 1985, Pete was also diagnosed with ALS and was told he had two years to live. Pete suffered and died from the complications of ALS. I lived. Why? Some believe God healed me. Pete died. Why?

If God sends miracles, God sends—by action or permission—the bad and evil stuff! Does a good God allow evil? If a miracle healed me, why wasn't Pete healed? We were both ministers. Many offered prayers for both of us. Why was I spared? Did I have more faith? I think not. Was I the better person? Pete, God, and I all know better. Did my friends have more influence with God and were able to arrange my healing? I don't know why Pete died or why I still live. I am convinced, though, that God was with both of us all the way. Pete died in God's grace, aware that God was with him. I am still alive and struggle to remain aware that I am living in God's grace; God is with me. With Pete, God struggled with the meaning and the unknown of his dying. With me, God struggles with the meaning and unknown of my living—for a while longer. God is good, loving, and present with us. But God is not all-powerful, at least not in the ways I thought. There are things God can't do for me, for you, for anyone. But God can and does do something more important. God is with us.

Perhaps that is another reason Thomas's question was so troubling. No one had ever raped me. In fact, everything bad that ever happened to me somehow ended up okay, even ALS! I was uncertain about a lot of things but something came alive in me that day in the spiritual values group with Thomas. I was not sure about the implications that experience held for me, but I sensed I was beginning a journey into a new and different kind of understanding of my life and God's part in it. What did it mean to consider that God was in me, experiencing what happened to me, that God somehow shared in all of my experiences, felt what I felt, enjoyed what I enjoyed, grimaced when I felt repulsion? What can this mean in terms of where God is when I mistreat and abuse a person? Was this a major part of the discomfort I experienced as I sat with Karen? Was it I who had as yet an unformulated premonition about where this concept of God might lead me?

Karen, like Thomas, Sarah, and Pete, had not been rescued from her fate. She did not have a testimony about how God had intervened and brought her out of the sexual hell she lived in for twelve years. Nor did she claim it was "all worth it now, because God had marvelously turned all that bad into some wondrous good." Karen was approaching a crucial juncture in her life if she was to achieve her goal to live in a manner that was radically different from the way she had lived in the past. She would need to change her thinking about some basic and dominant beliefs in her life—beliefs about herself. Intrinsic to this were her beliefs about God and evil, about grace and punishment.

Karen's church operated the elementary school she attended. Church activities had been a part of her childhood. They still were. But Karen, like many of her "sisters and brothers," found that the traditional and standard ideas about the all-powerful, loving God and the evil in this world left her with few answers and harder questions. The songs and sermons about a good and loving God who is all-powerful, all-knowing, and present to protect us at all times were totally out of touch with the way life really was for Karen. She had dealt with her secret wounds and religious beliefs by mentally separating them. This was not a conscious decision. Karen did not think much about the overwhelming inconsistencies between what she had been taught and what she experienced. When she did, she turned to a traditional answer, "We don't understand why these things happen, but someday we will." Karen found little comfort and no healing in this belief. But it was all she had, and she held it tightly.

Karen, like many people, was not interested in theological talk. She knew little about "that kind of stuff." However, some of Karen's theology kept her stuck in her life patterns. Her beliefs about God, sin, and guilt robbed her of power and hope that a faith and grace relationship with God offers. White or bluecollar people do not talk about such "stuff" as theology. Yet even the simplest questions we ask about everyday life speak about theology. A truck driver at the Little America's Truck Stop in Wyoming talks theology when he reads the newspaper headlines over his eggs and hash-browns. He mutters, "I don't understand things like that—nine- and ten-year-old boys molested and murdered. How can anyone do that to a kid? Anyone who does that ought to be shot on the spot. Don't arrest 'em, just shoot 'em. What's this world coming to? Things like that shouldn't happen. It just isn't right."

Whether a top executive, a school crossing guard, or a hospital chaplain, we are "doing theology" when we reflect on what happens to us and other human beings. The "whys, wherefores, and how comes" of our life events are questions about meaning and value and purpose. These are questions about good and evil and God (or no God). They are unavoidable when we encounter the really hard moments in life, when we come face to face with injustice and wrongs, the bad and evil things that happen to people. When we talk of these things, we are talking theology. The word theology comes from two Greek words which mean "God" *(theo)* and "reason" or "knowledge" *(logia)*. Theology is simply a way or method of speaking, of reasoning about God. Karen was speaking about God. She did not realize how interwoven was the way she spoke about God with the negative ways she lived her life.

"If God was in me," Karen continued, *"why didn't he do something? He is all-powerful and can do anything. He could have done something. I mean, he's God. If he was in your Thomas and in me, why didn't he help us?"* Her voice was tense, almost defiant.

We sat and looked at each other. Finally I spoke.

"Karen, it was impossible for God to stop what was happening to you, or Thomas, or Sarah. It was impossible for God to prevent your being raped." My voice trailed, *"Impossible...."*

"Huh? God can do anything. I've been told that all my life. Impossible? What do you mean, it was impossible for him to stop it? He is God. He can do anything he wants to do, any time he wants to. I don't understand."

I understood Karen's confusion. It isn't easy to change the way we

think about what we believe, even when what we believe is contradictory to our experiences and keeps us in a painful bind. Karen's
bind was clear:

A. She believed God is all-powerful, loving, and just.
B. She knew bad things happened to her when she was a
   child.
C. She believed she was bad and deserved what happened to
   her, otherwise the all-powerful, loving, and just God
   would have done something to help her.

Event B was a historical fact; it was Karen's experiential reality.
Since B could not be changed, Karen's well-being rested on her coming to terms with the relative truth of A and C. If C were true, then
there is, to some small degree, a balance—some justice. Indeed, this
is the way she had coped. If Karen was bad, then she could reason
that she deserved what happened to her. Karen often said, "I didn't
deserve to be born." She could still hear her mother's words, "I
should have had an abortion."

But if C were not true, then Karen faced a real problem. It is the
same difficulty that Job faced. Job, you remember, wished he had
never been born. If C is not true—precisely what Job contended
about himself—then it must be true with Karen as it proved to be
with Job. To change Karen's thinking about C demands a cor-
responding change in her thinking about A. If any part of C is not
true, then none of A could be true. Karen's spiritual and psychological health was tied to a change in her thinking about A and C.
But how could she change her thinking? Her economy of things fit.
For Karen, A and C were true: God is all-powerful, loving, good, and
just; she was bad and responsible for what happened to her, otherwise God would have protected and healed her.

Over the years Karen, in the same way as most orthodox religion,
developed a workable system of beliefs built out of her understanding
of the Bible, sermons, songs, and teachings she had heard. She
learned that there is a balance to the system of good and bad. It has a
simple equation: if evil or bad things happen to you, it is your fault
(punishment); if good things happen to you, it is God's fault (blessings); if a really bad thing happens to you and you don't deserve it, it
is kind-of God's fault (blessings in disguise, God teaching a lesson,
God arranging or allowing an opportunity to grow in character).

It was four or five months later. Karen stared at the childhood photographs posted on the easel in my office. They had become part of our sessions. Each week they sat there like silent partners in our work. Finally, Karen spoke.

"She was so small—"

As we studied the pictures of her at age four and five, seven and eight, Karen began to find it harder to blame that little girl for something someone else had done to her.

The Apostle Paul offers insights into the workings of the spiritual and psychological change which Karen faced: "Do not be conformed to this world [a particular way of thinking] but be transformed by the renewal of your mind [a new way of thinking] (Rom 12:2). Paul offers insight into the psychology of change. It begins with a mental and spiritual process. Literally, he is saying that transformation comes about when we change our minds about things, change the way we think. How? We do this by human decision and effort linked with divine inspiration and empowering possibilities. Clearly, one's understanding of God and how God relates to us is the key to this transformation. Some things we cannot change. We cannot control everything that does or does not happen to us. Not even God can do that. But we can change what we do and how we name what does or does not happen. That is the key to the way we live in and beyond the events of life.

"...very small. Very small," I replied. "Karen, do you really believe God could let a little girl be raped if it was possible to stop it?" I continued, "I know what I said sounds strange to you, but what if it is true? What if God could not stop your abuse? What if some of the things we were taught about God during our childhood were not accurate? Karen, I believe it was impossible for God to intervene in your abuse because God does not control human behavior. Not yours, not mine, not anyone's. God plays by the same rules we are subject to in this world. There is a very real sense in which God is at the mercy of our choices."

The idea that God is in control of our world and what happens to us is a basic part of most traditional and contemporary religious thinking. God governs everything that happens. It is precisely this kind of thinking about God that has contributed to the endless dilemmas of the Thomases and Karens of all time.

The average person has never read the works of St. Augustine, so it would surprise many to learn that his writings have influenced their ideas about good and evil. Augustine was one of the more prolific writers among the early church fathers. In the *City of God,* written in the third century, Augustine set out the underlying concepts for a great part of Protestant and Catholic thinking about how God relates to what happens to us. Augustine could not understand God apart from God's being in complete control of everything that happened, including the bad things that happen to a person. Writing on acts of evil and tragedies, Augustine said:

> ...for he [God] is called omnipotent on account of His doing what He wills, not on account of His suffering what He wills not; for if that should befall Him, He would by no means be omnipotent.... Therefore, whatsoever a man suffers contrary to his own will, he ought not to attribute to the will of men, or of angels, or of any created spirit, but rather to His [God's] will who gives power to wills.[4]

This line of thinking maintains the sovereignty of God and insists that God is all-powerful.[5] That is, whatever happens to any person is traceable to God. The presence of evil in the world challenges the common understanding of God's mercy and control over the world and human acts. The capacity for choice challenges any claims for humanity's innocence. But by stringent standards we must judge Thomas, Sarah, and Karen innocent of the evil they experienced. What happened to them was, in Augustine's words, contrary to their will and, consequently, they were not morally responsible for it. Their innocence challenges this view of the mercy and justice—the use of power—of both God and humanity. Can God be truly loving and just and at the same time be ultimately responsible for allowing the evil these innocent children endured?

The concept that God is in control of everything that happens to us is comforting and assuring for many people. For many others, though, it causes confusion and anguish. This is painful for those who suffer from the grave misdeeds of others and the random tragic events of nature. They draw the unavoidable conclusion that God did it or, for some unknown divine reason, allowed it. This shores up the premise that everything that happens is God's will. This is a simple approach that demands a simplistic, unquestioning, but fatalistic faith. It calls for a faith that must ignore the inconsistencies it sets up in the nature of God. For some, its simplicity is unacceptable in light of the statement it makes about God and how God treats us; it simply does not make sense. For me, it is a deeper form of blasphemy. Such a view makes us puppets dangling on the Divine Mover's strings. We might be free to jerk and jump about and exercise some freedom at the end of the string, but inevitably we are still under the control of the Puppeteer's strings. God holds those strings and ultimately the puppets move at the divine will. This is a kind of Freudianism whereby the one holding the strings—whether biological, psychological, or theological in character—controls the human person.

If God is omnipotent and actually in control of human events and the forces of nature, there can be no other possible answer: God could have prevented or stopped the hideous atrocities forced on Thomas and Sarah and Karen, but chose not to. Rape? Abuse? God wills or allows it? God has the power and capacity to stop it and does intervene—now and then? Thomas's question rages against this: "Where is the all-powerful God when I am powerless to avoid tragedy and to protect myself from the ravages of evil?"

"Standing by, watching..."
"Holding the victim while it happens..."
Sarah said, *"God was with me, within me—he, too, was being raped."*

This offered Sarah a new hope—the hope of a God who was not just over her, greater than her. It was the hope of a God who was with her, a part of what she was enduring, including her powerlessness over people and circumstances.

Sarah was not concerned that it was a radical concept. What had happened to her as a child was radical, and simplistic answers did not stand up in the face of her life experience. Sarah gained a different understanding of God. Finally she had a way of thinking about God that helped free her from anger and doubt. God was closer and more real than she had ever realized. God really did care about her. God was with her.

Karen was beginning to consider new possibilities concerning God's presence in her life, how God is the ground and source of our being (Acts 17). This does not change the reality of God. Rather, it expands one's understanding of how God relates to us. This view is grounded in the message of grace and the progressive understanding of the nature of God as recorded in the Bible and the experiences of men and women of all times. Concisely, God is unwilling and thus unable to control human experience. God is unable to control human experience because of the Divine choice to enter into a creative process with the creation. God is not some existential remoteness who has wound up the world like a toy and is out there somewhere watching to see how it will run. Nor is God a master manipulator, playing with the world like a kid with a remote-controlled robot. God has chosen to relate to our world in a creative process where Divinity can be a part of humanity. Creation is the expression of the Divine choice to enter into an ongoing process as opposed to accomplishing a single act.[6]

God chooses to be with us, is willing and able to enter into human experience, is living with us. God's "with-us-ness" is uniquely exemplified in the life, death, and resurrection of Jesus of Nazareth. It is ultimately expressed in the daily life and death of individual persons.

The Letter of James states that to know to do good and to fail to do it is a sin (4:17). If God has the power to protect innocent children from significant evil and does not, then, according to James's inspired understanding, God would stand judged by God's own command. Either God can stop evil and does not, or God does not stop it because God cannot. If God can stop evil and chooses not to do so, then God can willfully choose not to do good on some occasions and choose to do good at other times. This suggests that any means can be justified by a divine end.

But what if God is consistent? What if God consistently does not prevent or stop the evil people choose to do to each other because God is not free to stop it? What if human freedom to choose limits God's freedom to act in ways contrary to that choice? If this is true, God has chosen to be powerless in the face of human choice.

Sarah said, "God was in me." As Sarah was raped, she fixed her eyes on the crucifix hanging on the wall of the small staff room in the orphanage. She prayed to the "God on the cross" for help, but she found that God powerless. She prayed; she asked him to come down off the cross and help her—but nothing happened. He was unable to come off the cross and deliver her from the evil, sadistic actions of a perverted human mind. How reminiscent of David's words, "Lord, how long will you stand there doing nothing?"

Sarah's childish logic helped her understand why God did not help her. He was on a cross and could not help her. Two thousand years earlier he had been unable to stop his own crucifixion. How, then, could he possibly stop someone from raping her? At the time, Sarah was not capable of making that kind of symbolic connection, but she was living proof of the mysterious truth that was expressed at the crucifixion of Jesus: "He saved others; let him save himself if he is the Christ of God, the Chosen One...." "If you are the King...save yourself!" (Lk 23:35,37).

Many of the people who heard Jesus speak about salvation—about being saved—misunderstood him. In the Gospel accounts, it is obvious that even Jesus' disciples were slow to realize that Jesus was talking about spiritual salvation, not some kind of physical deliverance from the evils of their day; namely, the Roman conquerors.

When Jesus spoke of salvation, he referred to saving the soul or psyche—the essence and being of the human person. The word normally translated "soul" in the Gospels and Letters is the Greek word *psuch,* where we get the word psyche. Jesus once asked, "What shall it profit a man if he gain the world and lose his soul?" (Mt 16:26). "Soul" is literally "psyche." As a child, Sarah expected a physical rescue—to be saved. It didn't happen. But her God was not just standing around somewhere—waiting. How could he help her? He, too, was suffering—hanging on a cross. Even a child could understand that. To a child of twelve, a crucifix hanging on a wall was more than a symbol. As she grew older, Sarah would understand more about the meaning of the crucifix. She would never, however, understand less about the crucifixion and its meaning.

Sarah's God was powerless to help her change circumstances that were beyond her control. Still, Sarah could keep on believing in and praying to a God who understood what it was like to suffer innocently at the hands of evil. That kind of God understood pain and its demeaning cousin, suffering. God had not answered her prayers for help, but the image of that God on a cross gave her hope. God had not ignored her. The God on the cross was there, suffering, and like her was powerless to escape the evil in life. She did not find deliverance from her ordeal. But she did find the salvation of her psyche—soul.

Later Sarah began to understand more fully how God is powerless in the face of human choice. In fact, in the face of a human choice for evil action God is the most powerless. When a human person makes a choice to do evil, God does the only thing God can do—the one thing that only God can do: God enters fully into the experience; God is fully present—incognito—in the person, feeling, thinking, and absorbing the totality of the moment. These are some of the implications of Sarah's insights that were beginning to trouble me.

An underlying precept of most religious thinking is the belief in free will, the primary capacity and power humans have to make choices. This is central to the message of the Genesis creation story. Human beings are created and empowered with the freedom to choose, apart from animal instincts and unfettered by Divine control. This is symbolized in the creation story by the relationship Adam and Eve had with God. Adam and Eve represent the human race and were given the power to name the animals of creation. They had the power to choose how they would behave and, ultimately, to name the meaning they gave to their experiences. There is no greater power than to name the meaning of one's experience. As Frankl said, to choose how we will respond, how we will name the meaning of what happens to us, is the last human freedom.[7]

Sarah did not need an academic degree in order to understand. Her language was simple, based on an experience of faith. That was enough for her. Fortunately, one does not have to endure Sarah's trauma to understand the truth of her discovery.

Many today are caught up in a crisis of faith. They struggle to hold onto their belief in God in the face of evil and unpredictable life events. The discoveries of modern science perplex others, challenging long-cherished beliefs about our world. Some see inconsistencies between their beliefs about God and the way God relates to them and their neighbors in everyday life. They observe a dichotomy between the plenty in America and endless famine in much of the world. They once learned that God spoke and the universe was there—full grown and fixed. Yet, everything known today about the universe claims it is alive and, after billions of years, still in a creation process.

God is not a divine giant who does everything for us—that is, for some of us, some of the time. We must discover God, not as one who does miracles for us, but rather in the miracle that God lives life with us and is consistently with us in the midst of the inconsistencies of human experience. God is in human life, experiencing all that happens to us. God is always with us, encouraging, inspiring, affirming, luring us to go on, to live, to do—to be the good. Many today need a faith-understanding of God as the one whose power within helps and enables us. That power is there to save us, not *from* the evil of this world, but to save us *to meaning and purpose* in this world and the future.

Carl Jung did not consider himself a theologian, but his study of psychology and psychiatry led him to believe that God was involved in every moment of human experience. Jung expressed this conclusion in a statement carved into the stone arch over the entrance to his counseling office in Switzerland. All who came to him for therapy could see it. The Latin inscription read: "Vocatus atque non vocatus, Deus aderit" ("Summoned or not God will be present"). This statement is the foundation for Sarah's understanding of God. It is a silver thread in biblical history. We did not invite God into our world nor did we create God. God chose to be in our world and continues to be alive in it. God is with us in the mess of our world—individually and collectively. Here lies the deeper meaning of Sarah's statement. God does not control our lives but God is experiencing our life with us. We find this idea in Paul's declaration to the community leaders in Athens:

> "For the God who made the world and everything in it…does not live in shrines made by man….He is not far from each one of us, for in him we live and move and have our being" (Acts:17:24, 28).

Paul, like us, had trouble using finite words to explain the infinite. Nevertheless, a theme stressed in his writings is that there are no boundaries between the being of God and the being of humans; our lives are wed together. God is in relationship with us. Paul told the people of Athens, who knew nothing of Christianity and little of Judaism, that their existence was possible because of God's dynamic presence; that is, the human person does not exist apart from the very being of God—in God and with God we have our being. Our human existence is connected to and inseparable from God. Apart from God we have no being—we do not exist. Paul is not talking about individual awareness of the interconnectedness of God and the human person. In fact, he suggests that understanding of one's connectedness with God or the emotional experience of it may be absent. The Athenians believed in multiple gods, but they did not understand how what they called God was related to them.

Regardless of our understanding and awareness, God is with us. This is precisely what Paul pointed out to the Athenians. God was present in their existence but they did not recognize it fully nor understand the implications of the idea. According to Paul, God is the means and essence of our very existence, whether we are aware of it or not. The major purpose of religion is to enable us to become aware of the connectedness we have with God.

God who is present in my life and in yours has not entered into our lives as an impersonal, transcendent "Other." God enters personally into our human experience. God is not present as a bystander or a fellow traveler who from time to time carries us over the rough spots. God is more than a loving father who consoles and chastens us. The eternal God, who endlessly exists before and after the physical world of time and place, has taken up domicile in humanity, is cohabitant with humanity. This is not some "new age" pantheistic god or godness. God is alive in everything, but everything is not God. God is more than the sum total of the parts of this world. God, Paul notes, does not dwell in shrines or temples built by human hands, but in the center of human life.

For many people, God is apart and distant from their world and their life. Some classical religious views conceive God as immutable and unchanging. That is, human experience cannot affect God; we can do nothing that has a personal impact on God. God's perfections are understood as complete without a world, without you and me. So God is transcendent, totally other than and beyond the experiences and limitations of human reality. Such a God doesn't need to love or be loved. This idea of a perfect God has strong roots in the non-Christian Greek philosophy so prevalent during the period the Christian scriptures were written.

If God cannot personally enter into human experience, there is nothing of value for God in creating a world. This God is incapable of experiencing anything related to creation on any kind of personal level. This God is "impassible," immune to pain and suffering or any human emotions. God experiences the suffering of humans only through empathy. Using this logic, no human act can affect God. This makes God the ultimate computer who comprehends human suffering just as a computer reads electronic impulses and signals to arrange them into meanings. But it constructs a God incapable of experiencing the data or knowing any of its dynamic and affective impact.

Prayer has always been an important religious practice. To the surprise of some, prayer has gained the keen interest of many in the fields of psychology and medicine. In 1968 when Harvard cardiologist, Herbert Benson, began research on the physiology of meditation, little did he suspect that he would one day set off scientific debate on the health benefits of prayer. Benson and his fellow researcher, physiologist Robert K. Wallace, found that the repeated mantra replaced the arousing thoughts that otherwise keep a person tense during most waking hours. By the time he published his research in *The Relaxation Response,* a 1975 best-seller, Benson found that the simple, repetitive prayers all major religious traditions use create what he terms the relaxation response (RR). Benson discovered that the relaxation response is opposite to the stress reactions widely studied as the fight-or-flight response, an organism's defense against dangers. The results of RR are lower metabolic rate, slower heart rate, lower blood pressure, and slower breathing.[8] Benson continued his research on the effects of prayer and meditation on the physical health of a person. In 1989 he reported that "people who feel themselves in touch with God are less likely to get sick and are better able to cope when they do."[9]

Most religious groups emphasize two major categories of prayer: prayers of adoration and prayers of petition. The Bible and religious tradition place emphasis on the importance of praising God and making requests known to God. Yet, if God is totally removed from direct human experience and cannot be affected by it, what value can God find in our praise? What purpose is petitionary prayer? It cannot affect God. God won't experience pain or joy, pleasure or displeasure, or change of mind. In a world where everything is predetermined and known to God, prayer is meaningless. The value of prayer and praise in such a system is only in terms of the effect it has on the person who prays. The only purpose for prayer would be to encounter the unalterable will of God and to change one's desire and petition. The only purpose of praise and worship is to give adoration to a being who does not need it and cannot experience it.

Perhaps Sarah's experience sheds some light on another way of looking at prayer, another way of understanding how adoration and worship or blasphemy and sinning affect God and the human person. Sarah's idea focuses on God's relation to the world in terms of growing and expanding and becoming. The things we have discovered about our earth and our universe tell us we live in a "becoming" world. Our universe is not a static machinelike universe that has never changed. Conditions may seem stable and fixed but, in reality, everything in the universe is in a state of constant, sometimes microscopic, change. As part of our universe and our world, God is also becoming and expanding the Divine experience of humanity.

Many contemporary Christian theologians and scientists agree that God, as Norman Pittenger suggests, is absolutely "unsurpassable by anything."[10] However, while it is true that God cannot be surpassed by anything in creation, it is also true that God can increase in the richness of the Divine experience. God, as the Biblical records state, is a "living" God. In the fullest sense, this means that God increases the richness of the Divine experience through human relationships. Through the Divine involvement with the created order and humanity, God apprehends something that God has never experienced. The apex of this richness was in Jesus of Nazareth, the Christ. But the significance of a "living" God is found in the Divine capacity to share in, to interact with, to be in relation with individual and collective human experience.

Prayer is not intended to be the pleading of a child who tries to change his father's mind to get something he needs or wants. It is a conversational relationship with a God involved with our needs and wants on the experiential level. In prayer, one encounters the reality of what is, what can or cannot be. In that moment, God and I explore the realities and the possibilities of all three. This experience with God creates new possibilities of all three. This experience with God creates new possibilities in me and, consequently, in others. This relationship with God affects not only me but also, in varying degrees, the world. Because life and the world is open to creative advance, I can be different and things can be different in perception and in fact. Thus, prayer becomes an experience where one event—my experience with God—influences all other events—my interactions with others and theirs in kind. Prayer is truly an event that affects God and me in an ongoing, expanding way by all that happens between us. Thus the focus of prayer is to mesh with God, accepting life as it is and influencing it for the highest good. When a human joins God in prayer, the infinite possibilities that exist in God open to the finite possibilities that reside in a human. These possibilities include the desires, hopes, and aspirations of God and the human person. That kind of prayer is highly effectual. It enhances the human person and his or her perceptions; it enhances the Divine person as the expression of each finite experience becomes a part of God's experience. This kind of prayer can enhance the world and, at times, even change it.

The God described in the Bible is an empathic God involved in human experiences, feeling as humans feel. Moses said God experiences jealousy (Ex 20:5). John said God experiences loving (1 Jn 4:10). David said God experiences kindness (Ps 63). Paul said God experiences hate (Rom 9:13). The chronicler said God experiences anger (1 Kgs 11:9). Jesus said God experiences forgiving (Lk 23:34). These testaments describe God with emotions that seem responsive to human experience. The God of the Hebrews was a Holy Other, so holy that one dared not speak his name. Yet God was also understood in human characteristics. This is evident in the dominant trait of maleness attributed to God throughout the Bible. The biblical idea that God is present in all human experience progresses until it is fully revealed in the person of Jesus of Nazareth.

It is in this light that we can consider the nature of God's "powerlessness." What do I mean when I say God is powerless or helpless? Professor Bernard Lee states it well: "...there is something real in the character of God which makes it valid to speak positively about a helplessness in God."[11] There is a quality in the character and nature of God that makes helplessness and powerlessness primary in the Divine-human relationship. There is a powerlessness that is an unavoidable corollary of the character and nature of the human person. A clarion message of the biblical prophet and apostle alike is that God is *relational*. The inspired biblical record is an account of endless ways where God is involved in the experiences of human beings. The Bible is an inspired record of humanity's growing awareness of God's relatedness.

Central to the essence of relationship is a respect and allowance for mutual understanding and freedom. In the Genesis account, God gives Adam and Eve the ultimate freedom, the freedom to choose their actions. This ability to make an unfettered choice was part of the original structure in the relationship between Creator and creation. In the creation story God could not stop Adam and Eve from eating the fruit of the knowledge of good and evil. God's power has always had limits. To give a person a choice requires that one not violate the integrity of that gift. If I give you a gift, I relinquish control over it. If, somehow, I maintain control over the gift, it is not yours. I may, in fact, have loaned it to you. But I did not give it to you as a gift.

God had the power to create human beings free to choose who they will be and what they will do. By that very action—creation of human free will—God was "self-rendered" powerless in the face of every human choice whether that choice be good or evil. The Genesis story tells us that after Adam and Eve ate the fruit, God drove them out of the garden. But God did not abandon them. God went with them. They could not remain in the garden, but neither could God because wherever men or women go, there God goes.

Humanity's relationship with God has never depended upon our living in a Garden of Eden. After Eden, Adam and Eve—humanity— changed; they were no longer innocent. They understood the meaning of and the difference between good and evil. After the story of Adam and Eve comes the biblical account of a growing, developing world, a picture of an evolving and expanding understanding of who God is, and how we relate to one another. The drama of theological evolution is played out in the Bible's central character, Israel. It is important to note that God was with Israel just as with Adam and Eve. God walks with them, talks with them, and is a part of all they do. As we read the history of Israel, we begin to understand that God is with every nation, every person. God is with us in the mess we call life!

It is easy to emphathize with the thoughts Rabbi Richard Rubenstein expresses in his book, *After Auschwitz*. Rubenstein's efforts to reconcile the historical Jewish and Christian concepts of God with the events of Auschwitz have touched many. Referring to Rubenstein's work, Bernard Lee notes, "If God could have prevented the attempted genocide and slaughter of six million Jews (God's *chosen people*) and did not, then God has forfeited the right to be called the Lord of History."[12] When seen in the light of Eden, the matter is clear. God did not prevent the Holocaust because God could not prevent it. God could not veto the human choice at Auschwitz any more than in Eden. God did not cause or allow Hitler to kill Jews. Neither did God use Hitler to punish the Jewish people for their refusal to accept Jesus of Nazareth as the Messiah anymore than God used the "serpent" to tempt Adam and Eve to sin. But what God did at Auschwitz was the same as God did in Eden. In the creation story we don't find God around when Adam and Eve eat the forbidden fruit. God must have been "out of the office." But maybe not; maybe God was there more than Adam or Eve could understand or more than we dare to believe.

God lives within each of us, providing the personal urge or the invitational lure to good, presenting an ever-expanding reservoir of possibilities for good. Thus, God was in every act done by every individual and every nation who stood against the carnage of the individual and collective Auschwitzes in human history. God called the hearts and minds of men and women around the world to overcome evil with good. Lee points to this truth when he says of Auschwitz, "God had to stand outside the sanctuary of human freedom and helplessly watch the desecration...."[13] God, always helpless in the face of human freedom, was powerless to make the exterminators at Auschwitz act differently. If God was powerless to stop Adam and Eve from eating a bad apple even though it would have an impact on the human race for centuries to come, how can we claim God had the power to stop a Hitler from murdering millions of people? God could not undo creation and violate Adam and Eve's freedom to choose, their power to act. Likewise, God was helpless to stop Hitler's action even when it involved countless acts of gross evil. Cam Hanemann, a former student, expressed it well: "God will not manipulate my freedom or my unfreedom." Our own experiences bind us and God does not force us to be other than what we are. Psychological and spiritual wounds of incest bound Karen. She was not free to relate to God or others in open and loving relationships. God did not judge her but invited her to see new possibilities in herself and in others. God was in her, inviting her to new levels of self-acceptance and enjoyment in her relationships.

Rubenstein sees God as powerless in the "sanctuary of human freedom." But standing outside, helplessly watching, is not God's only option. Sarah and Rubenstein agree. God is unable to stop the "desecration." But there is more. God, unwilling to stand by and watch, enters into it with us. God has that power. Helpless to stop human action, God is committed to sharing it with us to the fullest. This is God's greatest power. This is what the Crucifixion was all about. God is and continues to be fully involved in human experience.

Someone said, "We are in this world together alone." The paradox is that we are in this world alone, together—alone together with God. A familiar quote about God's presence is Jesus' words "...where two or three are gathered in my name, there I am in the midst of them" (Mt 18:20). There is a less quoted apocryphal statement attributed to Jesus: "And where there is one alone, I say I am with him."[14]

Thomas asked, *"Where was God when I was raped."*

Sarah said, *"God was a little girl—in me—when I was raped."*

"The three victims mounted the chairs. The hangman placed the three necks in the nooses. 'Long live liberty!' cried the two adults. But the child was silent."

Those are the words of Elie Wiesel as he described the day he stood in the assembly yard of the concentration camp at Buna in World War II. All of the prisoners witnessed the hanging of three of their fellow Jews. They called the child a *pipel*, a term for a child with a refined and beautiful face. Wiesel said of this lad, "He was loved by all. He had the face of an angel."

As Wiesel stood there watching the execution, he heard a voice speak out from behind him.

"Where is God? Where is he?"

At a signal from the director of the camp, the three chairs were tipped over. Wiesel recalled:

Total silence throughout the camp. On the horizon, the sun was setting.

"Bare your heads!" yelled the head of the camp. His voice was raucous. We were weeping.

"Cover your heads!"

Then the march past began. The two adults were no longer alive. Their tongues hung swollen, blue-tinged. But the third rope was still moving; being so light, the child was still alive....

For more than half an hour he stayed there, struggling between life and death, dying in slow agony under our eyes. And we had to look him full in the face. He was still alive when I passed in front of him. His tongue was still red, his eyes were not yet glazed.

Behind me I heard the same man asking: "Where is God now?"

And I heard a voice within me answer him:

"Where is He? Here He is—He is hanging here on this gallows...."[15]

Karen sat pensively as she reflected on Wiesel's story. I waited. This was our 106th session. Or was it the 107th? My mind was not silent as our session ended that day.

The weeks passed. The foliage on Pete's Mountain across the canyon from my office window changed with the seasons. Karen continued in her work. At times it was slow moving—three steps forward, two steps back. But for the first time in her life Karen was seriously sorting out her feelings and beliefs about God and how God related to all that happened to her as a child. The limits of a God who was set in human characteristics and Greek philosophic images were beginning to expand. She was experiencing a new relationship with the God the Bible points to: the God, alive in human experience before the Bible was written; the God, still alive in human experience. She began to see how her abuse and her love/hate feelings toward men distorted her view of God.

As is true with most people, Karen formed her image of God when she was a young child. As an adult, Karen had never critically reviewed what she understood about God. For example, her image of a God who could be understood only in masculine terms began to fade. She was beginning to consider God as more than the perfect, superhuman father whose capricious wisdom is like that of TV's "Father Knows Best." Karen was discovering that the best images and symbols for God are, at best, just that: inadequate images and symbols. God, she was discovering, is more than the perfect man!

What Sarah is telling us is not new. It is a dominant theme of the entire Bible. If as Jesus often said, we "have eyes to see and ears to hear," the message is clear. *It is risky business being God.* If God really gives people the power to choose what they will do, how and to whom they relate, then God is taking a big chance because there are no guarantees, not even for God. God runs the risk that things will not always turn out for the best. They didn't at Eden or at Auschwitz.

The miracle is that God is still with us—in us. A statement attributed to Floyd Shaffer describes the miracle concisely: "The most powerful person in the world is the person who can give away power. This is what God did in the incarnation."

NOTES

1. Robert Frost, "Stopping by Woods on a Snowy Evening."
2. M. Scott Peck, *People of the Lie* (New York: Simon and Schuster, 1983), p. 62.
3. Elie Wiesel, *Night* (New York: Bantam Books, 1982), p. 3.
4. Augustine, *City of God*, Book V, Chapter X, Nicene and Post-Nicene Fathers, Vol. II (Grand Rapids, Michigan: Wm. B. Eerdmans, 1983), pp.92-3.
5. In traditional Christian theology, omnipotence is where "ability en-

tirely matches will." God can do anything God wills to do. God's power is not limitable. *Omnipresence* is "the quality or capacity" by which God is in all places at all times—there is "no place where God is not." God is "present to everything" but God is "not everything" as in pantheism. *Omniscience* is "the quality of knowing all." In traditional theism, God knows everything past, present, and future—pre-event as well as post-event. Many conclude that God "predestines" or "fore-orders" what God knows. *Twentieth Century Encyclopedia of Christian Knowledge* (Grand Rapids, Michigan: Baker Book House, 1955), pp. 818ff.

6. These ideas are rooted in process thought, a school attributed to Alfred North Whitehead (1861-1947). For additional insight see Lewis S. Ford, *The Lure of God* (Lanham, Maryland: University Press of America, 1985); American Academy of Religion, *Two Process Philosophers: Hartshorne's Encounter with Whitehead*, AAR Studies in Religion 5, 1973; John B. Cobb, Jr. and David R. Griffin, *Process Theology: An Introductory Exposition* (Philadelphia, Westminster Press, 1976).

7. Viktor E. Frankl, *Man's Search for Meaning* (Boston, Beacon Press, 1963).

8. Herbert Benson and Miriam Z. Clipper, *The Relaxation Response* (New York: Avon, 1976).

9. *Psychology Today*, October 1989.

10. Norman Pittenger, *Catholic Faith in a Process Perspective* (Maryknoll, New York: Orbis Books, 1981), p. 6.

11. Bernard Lee, "The Helplessness of God: A Radical Re-appraisal of Divine Omnipotence," *Encounter*, Vol. 38, No. 4 (Autumn 1977), p. 325.

12. *Ibid.,* p. 329. Parenthesis added.

13. *Ibid.,* p. 329.

14. Laurens Van der Post, *Jung and the Story of our Time* (New York: Vantage Books, 1975), p. 189.

15. Wiesel, *op. cit.,* p. 61ff.

CHAPTER FIVE

THE DEMAND:
God, Grace, and Gratuitousness

What do we do when things don't turn out for the best? This question concerns much of life and, in reflecting on it, I realize how much I have lived my life in answer to it. I do not suggest that nothing in life ever turns out right. But facts strongly suggest that something about the human condition favors things going sour for most of us much of the time.

This is a hard lesson to learn. We make mistakes and, at times, use faulty judgment. Add to this the ever-present reality that we live in a community of other human beings who are also given to faulty judgments and misbehavior. We may strive to be flawless, but we just can't be God.

So what does a person do? We can't control the world. We do our best and learn to live with our efforts. This is the basic Christian message. What happens to us doesn't matter; the presence of the grace of God in all that happens makes the difference. "For it is the God who said, 'Let light shine out of darkness,' who has shone in our hearts.... We are afflicted in every way, but not crushed; perplexed, but not driven to despair;...struck down, but not destroyed..." (2 Cor 4:6-9).

I learned this from Ira Lollis when I was a kid. Ira was a quiet, gentle man with a Bob Hope nose. He often poked fun at his nose to entertain kids. He had one goal: to keep kids like me off the streets. I understand now that he was subtly preparing us to meet the challenges in the streets of life. Ira was director of the Boys' Club and the boxing coach in Hot Springs, Arkansas, my home town. I loved boxing; it was safer than street fights and merited jackets and trophies for being good at having fun. As a young pugilist, I learned the skills to defend myself and to trade punches with the best boxers around. Ira taught me about right crosses, left hooks, and ways to win in the boxing ring. I put my boxing gloves aside many years ago, but I still integrate into my life the lessons Ira taught me during my workouts.

I have a poignant childhood memory of something Ira said to me just before a boxing match. As he laced up my gloves he said, "Horace, you'll do your best tonight but remember one thing. Two of you are going into the ring and only one can come out a winner. But neither of you has to come out a loser." Ira was not a perfect man, but he was a gracious man. He understood the inspiring, healing power of grace. Interested in my winning and losing, he was even more interested in how I handled either one.

Perhaps that is where the real turning points in life are found—how we deal with those moments when we do not come out a winner, or worse, when we are knocked completely out of the ring. It is then that we face the stigma of being a loser. Others may have the authority to name us a winner, but the power to name ourselves a loser resides in our own hearts and minds. Losing a boxing match did not make me a loser or a worthless person. Likewise a person who is raped is not bad or worthless.

Eden didn't turn out for the best. Things went badly awry, as did Auschwitz and Vietnam. This same pattern continues to appear in human experience.

Where is God when I don't win? when the referee turns his head and I am beaten half to death? when there is no referee at all and I am abused, even raped? God is in the same place doing the same thing as in Eden, Auschwitz, and the bedrooms of Thomas and Karen. God is present in each of us, feeling what we feel, inviting us to live in spite of it. God urges us to see the possibility for light in darkness, for life in death, for living with or rising above changing circumstances. God is saying, "He beat you, hurt you, raped you. But you are more than what happens to you—good or bad. You do not have to let them defeat you; you are more than anything that happens to you. You can be bigger than any wrong, stronger than any weakness. You can make it! You can!"

God is within us calling us to faith, to hope, luring us to go on living, to believe that there is meaning in life despite what happens to us. When things happen that we have no power to change, God experiences it with us. At that moment all the power of the universe is at our disposal to do the one thing that only we can do: rise above it, live through it, give meaning to our experience, find purpose in life in spite of or because of what has happened.

We have lived too long with the erroneous belief that God changes things. We've made God into something God is not, "a fixer of things," the magical genie of those who rub God the right way. God does not change things or circumstances. God does change people. God's grace is not addressed to circumstances and events. Rather God's grace is addressed to people as they face life events and live in their circumstances. We witness the presence and power of God when a person's spirit is changed and empowered to live with meaning and purpose, come what may. The perpetration of evil is proof of the depravity of humanity. Rising above evil, transcending it, is proof of human goodness inspired by divine grace.

In his Second Letter to the Corinthians (12:8-9), Paul asks God to remove a serious and aggravating physical problem. God's response was simply, "My grace is sufficient...." God did not respond to Paul's request with a yes or no. Rather, God seemed to say, "Paul, I don't change things. I give grace for people to handle all things." God's grace is presence and involvement in one's life; but God does not guarantee any change.

This is God's power, to grace us with possibilities and inspiration. Scripture calls this the image of God living within us. This is God's creative work continuing in each of us. This is the true redemptive work of Christ finding resurrected fulfillment in our lives. It is in these moments of grace that we are truly born again—resurrected from death to life.

Chaplain Hal Hingst tells of a visit with Pete Zagel shortly before his death. In response to Hal's question, "How is it going?" Pete said, "Hal, it is all grace—grace."

Humanity's response to evil is law and force. God's response to evil is grace and love. We cannot live without laws, and laws require enforcement. Being human, that is the way we do things. But will we ever accept the fact that God is not one of us? God is not a higher form or a better model of humanity. God is a totally different model; the divine way of dealing with human evil is radically different from ours.

God's response to Eden, Auschwitz, Vietnam, and the sinful blunders in my personal life is grace. God bless all the Ira Lollies in the world, for they are reservoirs of God's graciousness. They are the conduits of God's grace in concrete human interactions. Yet all of them combined make but a thimbleful of the measureless ocean of God's grace. God's response to human experience is the most difficult thing for us to comprehend. Although we will never fully understand it, with hope we may come to accept it.

The essence of grace in biblical terms is the unmerited favor of God. The word grace (*charis,* graciousness) expresses the nature and quality of God's disposition toward humanity (see Lk 2:40; Eph 2:5). The concept encompasses love, mercy, kindness, and unconditional, universal acceptance. Implicit in these words is the awesome and incomprehensible facet of grace which Gustavo Gutierrez calls gratuitousness.[1] Gratuitousness is an attitude or quality of character that affects and precedes action. It is a predetermined frame of reference from which all actions generate and the point of reference which establishes relationships. It is the quality of relationship or action that emerges freely from the giver without justification, reason, or prescribed self benefit. God's grace is not limited to one act or a group of actions taken in the past. On the contrary, it is an ever-present attitude and an ongoing relationship with us.

The structure and content of God's essential nature is gratuitousness. God does not extend love to us because of who we are or what we do. Instead, God gives it to us because of who God is. God's love is not a power to protect us from bad or a demand to make us behave. God's love extends to us in grace regardless of our behavior. God's nature is to be gracious; we can do nothing about it. We cannot barter for God's grace nor can we conspire to limit it. It is there. God's grace, in the truest sense, is a disinterested grace. That is, God is not duty-bound to be gracious as a reward for our goodness; God is gracious because of the unchangeable, the unalterable nature of God to be gracious. Just as God is powerless to interfere with our free will, so we are powerless to interfere with God's grace.

Religious teaching often centers on the immutability of God. We assure ourselves that God is the same yesterday, today, and forever, yet we speak of God's being kind to some yesterday, unkind to others today, and damning others tomorrow. We base God's various responses on our behavior. We ascribe God's response to us as loving and kind if we are good, judging and damning if we are bad. Thus God is seen as blameless in the damning; it is our fault. We forget that God's gratuitous nature does not change regardless of who does what, where, or when. God is the same yesterday, today, and forever. The sameness is God's grace!

God is in our corner whether we are right or wrong. Many find this hard to accept. The early followers of Jesus had problems with this idea. His disciples point to a blind man and ask if his sins or the sins of his parents caused his blindness. Jesus' response to this question is clear. "It was not that this man sinned, or his parents, but that the works of God might be made manifest in him" (Jn 9:3).

There are two interesting aspects of this statement. First, the word "works" is plural. This is important because the major focus dwells on Jesus' work of healing the man (curing his blindness). However, the heart of the issue is: Why is this man blind? Jesus' disciples pose a question about the meaning of suffering. What Jesus said is more crucial to us today than what he did that day two thousand years ago. Jesus answers a deeper question which addresses the meaning and purpose of life itself. Second, the word translated "works" does not refer specifically to any clearly defined action or to the performance of any specific function; that is, eating, sleeping, selling a car, or healing a blind man. It refers to activity in general and could be translated as activities or a course of action—even the way one lives one's life.[2]

Jesus' statement does not relate to the action that is about to happen—a healing. If this were the point, he would have said something much more appropriate such as "This man is blind so that I can demonstrate the work of God in healing him." This would support traditional theological understanding about the purpose of sickness and suffering. It is interesting that Jesus' disciples focused on a possible moral cause of the man's blindness. A short time later when people learned the man had gained his sight, they were preoccupied with the credentials of the person who helped him. They asked, "Was he healed in accordance with the orthodox theology governing such procedures?" It is evident from the story that both groups missed the meaning of Jesus' words and the purpose of his action.

The word "works" does not connect with the single action Jesus takes. It is plural. Thus it is more reasonable to see that it related to the man and his life experiences as a person born blind. The man's blindness was not based on sin—his sin or the sin of his parents, nor on the rationale that it gave Jesus the opportunity to give him sight. He was not born blind so that he would eventually meet Jesus on the streets of Jerusalem and be healed. He was not a special pawn on the chessboard of the cosmos waiting for the right moment when God would move him from blindness to sight. While there is no explanation for his blindness, the actual cause is immaterial. Jesus expressed the only potential purpose in his explanation: *that the workings, the activities of God in a human life might be expressed.* The works of God Jesus referred to were done by the man born blind, not by Jesus.

God was *in* the blind man. God was living in and through the everyday experiences of this blind person. As that man lived out his life, he gave expression and meaning to his awareness of God (or lack of it) in his life. In him, God was alive and coming into the world. Every day, in every event, God was inviting him to see possibilities in his blindness, calling him to live the fullest life possible under the circumstances. His circumstances were not the result of God's decision to make him blind. Blindness, as with all human conditions, is the result of the development of humanity and of living within the physical world.

We live in an orderly and predictable world. Scientists can calculate the movement of stars and planets centuries before their light becomes visible to us. Yet this world is filled with chance and unpredictability. At any given moment an earthquake can occur without warning, destroying a whole city and killing thousands of people. Or in any sexual act, egg and sperm can unite, chromosomes can combine and result in an unpredictable human experience. Why was the man born blind? Because being born is a risky event. It always has been and always will be. Blindness is but one of the risks of being human.

Given the development of health sciences in the twentieth century, if that man had been born today, he might have been born with normal sight. Normal vision would certainly have affected his life. But blindness does not determine the kind of person one becomes. Intangible qualities such as courage, integrity, internal strength, goodness, and God-likeness chart the way for the kind of life one lives, and give purpose and meaning to that life.

God was not invested in the man's blindness nor his sight. It was the man—his will, his spirit, his life. God was present in him long before Jesus came to town. The man faced the same kind of dilemma after his healing as he did before. Certainly, many things about his life were different. He had to face new possibilities, different opportunities, and the demands of new responsibilities. Win, lose, or draw, he had to name the purpose and meaning of his life. He alone was the judge to render that decision.

When we read the Bible, we often are so attracted to the miracles that we miss the miraculous. It is a miracle that Jesus put mud on a man's eyes and hours later that man could see. Is it not a miracle, too, that an ophthalmologist uses a scalpel or a laser beam to remove a cataract from a person's eye and within hours severely diminished vision becomes normal? Yet, greatest of all is the miracle that a physically blind or sighted person can see possibilities, can find meaning and purpose in life regardless of what happens to them. It is indeed miraculous when a man or a woman crawls out of the chaos of human degradation, stands upright and lives with dignity and love and hope, names the world good and works to make it better. At that moment the words of Jesus come alive, the works of God are displayed.

To paraphrase words of Irenaeus, the glory of God is the human person fully alive. Regardless of circumstances, such a person reveals the works of God.

At times the miracles in the Bible are difficult to understand. When something outside the natural order occurs, we call it a miracle. Even when something unexpected happens that is a part of the natural order, we still term it a miracle. Lightning strikes a man standing by a tree. He should be dead. Instead he is burned only slightly. We say it's a miracle that he survived.

The Gospels reveal that Jesus performed at least thirty-three miracles. Some people doubt that these events actually happened. Others insist that these events are examples of what God can and will do if a person has enough faith. I believe that miracles do occur. Things we cannot explain do happen. Some people with terminal disease do not die for some unknown reason. Growths disappear without surgery; the visually impaired regain sight without treatment; cancer cells vanish without radiation or chemotherapy. These are the rare exceptions to the so-called normal experience. We cannot prove why or how they happen. There just is no consistency to such events. We may try to recreate the circumstances when such a miracle occurs, but we cannot be sure of the same results. Some day we may discover that this so-called miracle is but a part of the created order and human experience. That will not make it less miraculous. It is normal for a scratch on a child's hand to heal within a few days, with or without a Band-Aid and a kiss to make it well.

It is natural for scratches on the human body to heal. Yet no scientist can explain why this happens. Scientists describe what happens in the healing of a scratch, but they do not know why it happens. What makes it natural—and normal—for a scratch to heal? Where do the cells get the inducement for the movement? What force urges healthy cells to overcome unhealthy ones? Why does this work at times while not at other times? God's presence and grace are at work. On an elementary level God invites our cells to wholeness. But at every level God is consistent. God will not—cannot—force a single cell to behave contrary to its will. God does not change cells but God enables people to change. When people change, miracles are but a part of the possibilities God's grace opens up to us.

Many assume that every person Jesus tried to heal was cured, that he was successful in every event we find recorded in the Bible. A reasonable assumption indicates that not all of his activities were written down. In fact, Jesus was not successful in Nazareth. Matthew tells us that Jesus did no "mighty works" in his hometown because of their "unbelief" (13:30). Belief or faith was not always a factor in the miracles recorded in the gospels. The blind man in John's Gospel is a prime example. He doesn't know Jesus and doesn't express any kind of faith in him until several hours or days later.

The focus on Jesus' miracles has changed radically over the past two thousand years. The main emphasis of traditional theology is on the miracles themselves and the methods or means by which they can be repeated. This is unfortunate and leads to grave misunderstandings of how God is present and active in our lives. To reiterate, miracles do occur. They did five thousand years ago; they still do today. That they happen is not the point. The point is that we cannot control or predict them. The only thing consistent about them is that there is nothing consistent about them. They occur when people pray; they occur when people don't pray. They happen to Christians; they happen to nonChristians. They occur in the lives of Jews and in non-Jews. They are found in the experiences of the faithful Buddhist and the nonBuddhist. Wherever you find God's children—good or bad—miracles happen.

We can draw some conclusions about miracles. Three factors are consistent in miracles. First, healings or miracles are the exception in the normal pattern of human life. Second, they are unpredictable and cannot be guaranteed. Third, the individual gives the only genuine meaning or purpose ascribed to them. That is true of everyone. The true meaning or purpose of our health or sickness, our life, or death is the one we give it. We do not determine what happens to us but how we live with what happens.

The four inspired accounts of Jesus' ministry give another important insight about this issue of miracles and the meaning we give them. Many facets of Jesus' activities bothered some religious and socio-political leaders of his day. Jesus' critics were not too troubled about the miracles he performed. They had no problem believing unexplainable healings. Such things had always occurred. They knew the stories about Elisha's healings. They believed Elisha even brought dead people back to life (2 Kgs 4:18 and 13). The miraculous was not news and contemporary historians referred to numerous healers throughout Judea. Jesus' audience was aware that the multiplication of the loaves and the raising of the dead were part of their tradition and beliefs. The heavenly manna of the Exodus story illustrated God's care for his people through the miraculous multiplication of insufficient rations. The great prophet Elijah brought the son of the widow of Zarephath back from the dead (1 Kgs 17). Elisha did the same for the Shunammite's son (2 Kgs 8). Jesus' wondrous deeds, in line with the acts of the prophets, should have brought him favor with anyone who knew the history of God's dealings with humanity—but for two things.

The center of controversy was not Jesus' way of healing nor was it what Jesus did that troubled his critics. Rather, it was when he did it and why he did it. How was Jesus different? What made him different from the other healers and itinerant prophet-teachers? What he did was done as an extension of God's grace. He did not receive payment as did the other healers of his day. No one could do anything to earn his touch, merit his help, or deserve his encouragement. Who he was and what he had was offered freely, even indiscriminately at times. This was a problem to many. They believed God caused people to be blind, or lame, or emotionally disturbed because they were sinners. Thus when Jesus healed as an expression of God's grace he was violating the Divine order. The prevailing theology decreed that the man was blind because God wanted him to be blind. When Jesus heals, then, the reaction is not to the miracle but to disrupting God's will and doing so in God's name.

This was the major reason the protectors of the orthodox theology accused Jesus of healing by "the power of Beelzebul," the chief among evil spirits (Mt 12:24). Jesus' random healing seemed an act of capricious grace. According to the theology of the day, one might earn the favor of God, but God did not give this favor out at random—and never freely. It may seem strange that there was a spontaneity and randomness about much of the good Jesus did. It is natural to believe that if the blind man had overslept that morning or been sick with the flu, he would very likely have lived and died blind. It is hard to accept chance as a basic part of our world. We would rather have a God who is gracious to some and ungracious to others than live in a world where good and bad are, so to speak, up for grabs. We are uncomfortable in a world where God is gracious to all, where graciousness is not measured in good and bad events. It's troubling to think that God's grace is found in the intimate and consistent presence of God in and with us. Was God expressing this in the words of the ancient sage? "Again I saw that under the sun the race is not to the swift, nor the battle to the strong, nor bread to the wise, nor riches to the intelligent, nor favor to the men of skill, but time and chance happen to them all" (Eccl 9:11).

Jesus related everything in life to the gracious presence of God in human experience. Jesus saw God everywhere—in the lilies of the field, in the generous action of a member of a minority group, in the tax collector who became a philanthropist. But the keynote was always the same: the capacity and willingness of the people to see God in their everyday experiences, not in what happened to them.

Jesus told his disciples that they did not know the meaning of the man's blindness. Only the man and God knew this. The purpose in his blindness was the same as in all human experiences, that the "works of God might be manifest in him." How? By his living every day as a blind person. God did not choose to make him blind any more than God chose to make me short. But God did choose to live with him and experience all the challenges that a blind man would encounter. That is true for each of us. Regardless of genes, vitamins, circumstances, and choices, our lives are prime opportunities for the works of God to find expression. God loves us and invites us to be an expression of that divine love and grace in our lives.

We are not alone in this universe. God is a part of our world, not out there in some fixed position wanting to relate to us. God is with us, within us, inviting us to live life to the fullest. Often the deprived and underprivileged of the human race live the fullest and most meaningful lives while the advantaged and wealthy find life boring and meaningless. The meaning of life is not outside us nor is it in things or other people. The manifestation of God's works is *in us;*

this is the great gift that God gives us.

It is tragic when a Thomas or a Karen is raped. Such evil acts should not happen, but they do; they are the consequence of human choice. But the greater tragedy is that these victims miss the presence of God within them in their tragic experience. God is there with them, feeling and sharing in it. God is with them, calling them to live and become more than the tragedy they encountered. Why can't we trust God's grace? Why do we insist that God behave the way we do? Why can't we accept God as God even if it does not fit our biblical interpretation and theological tradition? We devote so much theological energy to make everything fit our Western logic. After spending six months as chaplain in the Persian Gulf War, I was convinced that this is one of our sins. We forget that biblical peoples were peoples of paradox and mystery. The Middle Eastern mind, filled with mystery and paradox, gave us the Bible; the Western mind organized it, clarified it, and made it contemporary. I wonder, what was lost? What was gained?

We are determined that everything we read in the Book of Exodus must be consistent with John's Gospel. But the authenticity of the revelation about God over five thousand years ago is different from the understanding of that revelation today. We know more about the nature of God today than Abraham did. Paul points to Abraham as an example of simple faith and the founder of a nation. But the writings of Paul make it clear that Abraham did not comprehend much about the nature of God and the way God relates to humanity.

The inspired records of God's dealings with ancient Israel are filled with prime examples of their confusion regarding God's grace and presence. When Israel experienced a defeat, they concluded God was not with them. When they won a battle, they believed God was with them. The Israelites' understanding of God was far better developed than that of their contemporaries, but still very much in process, even naive and primitive at times. Lewis S. Ford gives a good example of this in *The Lure of God*. He reminds us:

> Faced with the many gods of antiquity, the biblical tradition took an approach that…did not initially insist upon their nonexistence. The injunction was clear and practical, "Thou shalt have no other gods before me." This is primarily a vow of fidelity…[3]

At the time of the Exodus, Israel believed there were many gods.

The writer of Judges points out that Yahweh was God along with Chemosh, the god of Ammon (11:22-24). King Solomon recognized a plurality of gods when he built temples on the Mount of Olives for Chemosh, the depraved god of Moab, and Molech, the vile god of the Ammonites (2 Kgs 23:13). Moses, Joshua, and Solomon believed in the existence of many gods but there was one supreme and superior God—Yahweh—who was the God above all other gods.

The first commandment does not warn the Israelites against believing in many gods, but they are admonished to have no other god before or ahead of Jehovah. The Hebrews understood that God was calling them to fidelity. At the time of the Judges, Yahweh was conceived as one of many tribal deities. Yet less than six hundred years later, the writer of Isaiah declares the doctrine of monotheism. There is a new awareness in the Hebrews' understanding of God. The Lord God is the one and only God who is creator of the world and redeemer of Israel. To state it simply, the Bible clearly records a progressive and developmental understanding of God. God's self-revelation was not immediate and at one specific moment. It was an ongoing and continuous event.

This development carries the fundamental theme that God is not the cause of events but is a part of these events only as we experience them. God's grace is not a protective shield that we can hide behind; it is the divine intention of good toward us revealed by participation in life with us. God is not invested in changing anything that happens to us. God is invested in us—in our growth, development, and changes. "Emmanuel," the angel said to Joseph. "God is with us" (Mt 1:23). That presence means there are limitless possibilities available to inspire and energize us under any circumstances. For many, this idea calls for a radical rethinking of who God is. This is especially true when we reach adulthood only to discover that our concepts of God are still those we developed as children. To change what we believe about God may bring about the feeling that we are making God something less than who God is.

I recall an editorial on inclusive language that Chuck Colson wrote years ago. He was upset because critics were insisting he use more inclusive language in his addresses. He commented that one of the dangers in inclusive language is that it "...could eventually blur our understanding of who God is." He added:

All language about God is symbolic. Though God is evoked by female images in Scripture, male images predominate. This does not mean God is masculine. But if we strip the masculine of its symbolic significance we strip our understanding of God as well.[4]

"We strip our understanding of God." How ironic! Language that expands instead of restricts, symbols that enhance rather than limit are seen by some as stripping and blurring. It seems we do not want God to be too nonhuman. We want God to be different from us, but we also want God to be a perfect one of us—a perfect man, a perfect kind of human father. The predominance of symbolic language in Scripture is masculine and the logic is that God wants us to think of the eternal Divine predominantly as a him.

It is amazing that there are any nonmasculine images for God in the Bible. This is proof that God was luring the writers toward an inclusive, expanding understanding of the nature of God. In the male-dominated world of the Bible, one can hardly expect even inspired men to express their understanding of God apart from their powerful cultural conditioning. In many ways, the culture has remained unaltered as we approach the twenty-first century. In some ways Freud was right. We do seem to have an inescapable "father (male) complex."

The result of noninclusive language about God is, in the words of J.B. Philips, "a god who is too small."[5] The major problem with rejecting inclusive language is not that it leads to the insulting and degrading of women. Rather, the use of exclusive language results in a distortion and sacrilege of the person of God. The symbols we use for God limit our images of God. God is neither him nor her. God is, as Jesus said, more than human (Jn 4).

We need to be stripped of some of our understanding of God; our vision needs to be a bit blurred. This demands faith; we might be forced to see God as something more than a crystal clear mirror where we marvel at the enhanced perfection of our own reflection. This is the reason so many are devastated when bad things happen to good people. If we dare open our eyes to what life is really like outside our cozy narrow beliefs, the realities of life will strip away some of our understanding of God and of ourselves. That is the moment of truth, the moment when we choose to believe in a God who is not contained within our limited views.

One of the participants in Howard Clinebell's video series, "Growing Through Loss," shared her need for God to be a superhuman kind of God. The six-part video program documents the experiences of six survivors of significant loss as they work through their grief. In the group is a woman whose name is Karen. The Karen in the video survived the deaths of most of her family in a short period of time. As she talks of her losses, she speaks of her struggle with the reality that she has to face; that is, the fact that God is not the way she wants God to be. She is being stripped of some misunderstanding of who God is!

During a role play in the video, Clinebell has Karen engage in a dialogue with God. She speaks for God and for herself. She speaks first to God.

Karen: God, I want to know you are in control. I'm not sure you are. I'm really sort of shaken by that…. God, I am afraid. In a way I'm afraid that you've caused some of this to happen, and I'm not sure why. But at the same time, I'm afraid that you didn't cause it to happen and that you don't have control…. I'm not sure how to deal with that.

God: Karen, I am God and I do love you and I do care for you. Even though it (death) has come in big bunches, it will come to all people in one way or another. It's not a punishment and it's not because of anything special you have done or not done. It is just part of the order of things.

Karen: That makes a lot of sense…. I guess maybe what you want of me is to stop trying to play God and trying to figure it all out.[6]

The Karen in the video had lost her husband and several important family members. Her suffering challenged her understanding of God. She had lost loved ones who could not be brought back to life. The Karen sitting in my office had also lost family members and relationships, not because they died but because of abuse. More tragic yet, because of the abuse she had lost parts of her self and normal childhood experiences. These likewise could never be brought back to life.

Karen was on time as usual. We both sat motionless. She stared at the four pictures posted on the easel opposite her chair. She was four years old in the large one; two and six in two of the smaller ones.

The small snapshot bothered her the most. It showed only her head and shoulders. In it she was surrounded by several members of her family. The silence continued.

I am usually quite comfortable with silence in a counseling session, but during sessions with Karen I frequently had difficulty allowing the silence. I often had the impulse to speak, to draw her out, to help her move on with her life. It is hard at times to let people make their own choices and to sit with them in those choices. I was committed to honoring (allowing) Karen's choices and would maintain a healthy therapeutic distance in our relationship. I would not force my needs or will on Karen. To do so would be a subtle kind of rape.

In my mind, respecting Karen's space and her right to choose how and when she would change was "therapeutic grace." A friend and former colleague, Father Tony DeConcelous, often refers to the counseling relationship as a relationship of grace. What many critically call aloofness or indifference in a counselor may, in reality, be a small taste of disinterested grace. Carl Rogers termed this "unconditional positive regard"—an effort to honor the other person's individuality and integrity as a human being—his or her "self."

I prided myself in the thought that I would not impose my will on Karen. I was genuinely interested in her uniqueness and would let her make her own choices. I cared about her—yes, loved her—to the extent that I would not violate her person.

As I reflected, I realized that my thoughts were not only idealistic, they were also not true. I did not have the power to do some things in my relationship with Karen. At the top of the list, I would not let Karen kill herself or anyone else. Part of the contract with Karen clarified some things I would do if she attempted to harm herself or others. There was little I would not do if she made certain choices. I would not just sit with her and invite her not to do certain things. Under some circumstances, I would violate her free will and her rights to be human. I would see that she was hospitalized against her will if that was necessary to assure her safety.

As I thought more about this, I realized that my attitude toward Karen was much like the way many think God should be toward us. I began to realize that under certain circumstances I wanted to act like God and control Karen. Why? I can name many reasons. But the major reason is that I was, to a degree, legally and morally responsible for Karen. This was true but my own needs were a major part of that decision. Actually, there are times when I have difficulty valuing Karen's free will and self-choice above my own needs. If I were God, I would ultimately run the world the way I wanted. I was aware that I could not remain committed to Karen no matter what she did; there were limits. Only a God who is powerless to act ungraciously can truly remain gracious to all persons in all circumstances. That is the kind of love Paul hints of in his First Letter to the Corinthians.

Love is very patient and kind, never jealous or envious, never boastful or proud. It is never haughty or selfish or rude. Love does not demand its own way. It is not irritable or touchy. It does not hold grudges and will hardly even notice when others do it wrong. It is never glad about injustice, but rejoices whenever truth wins out (13:4-7).

We continued to sit quietly while Karen studied the photographs. I observed her closely, noting each slight facial movement. Karen ignored my suggestion that we begin the hypnosis session. She continued to stare at the pictures.

  "She was so little, so skinny," Karen said softly. There was a gentleness in her voice I had not heard before.
  "She couldn't protect herself."

I voiced my agreement and continued to wait, to listen. Karen looked better that evening than she had in weeks. Her hair was neat, pulled back and to one side in good taste but with a touch of flare. Her makeup was delicate and balanced. It was the first time in a month that she had worn makeup. Karen wore her feelings in her appearance. I had learned that Karen's appearance had a bearing on the silence I would encounter in each session. When I observed Karen that evening, I had a moment of déjà vu.

Working with a person who is a genuine multiple personality brings on a level of awareness that never leaves. Several things about Karen reminded me of Laura, one of six personalities within the person known as Michelle. Michelle and Karen were victims of sexual degradation and the kind of abuse that can occur in significantly dysfunctional families. Karen's abuse, however, was more extensive than Laura's because it involved so many people, it began at a younger age, and was marked by constant psychological conditioning.

A common coping technique that a victim of severe sexual abuse often uses is called "splitting." To endure the physical and mental torture, a child simply goes "somewhere," or becomes a totally different person in his or her mind. Mentally, the child will disassociate herself from what is occurring. Children are far more capable of this than are adults. Some splitting is so drastic that it becomes permanent and the child splits mentally into several personalities. Each personality becomes a separate integrated entity within him or her. Karen had read the story of Sybil, who experienced sixteen different selves.[7] Because of the severity and duration of Karen's abuse, I was alert to signs of a multiple personality. Hints from time to time suggested this, but I found no clear indicators.

Karen often sat with me—shattered and depressed at times but fairly integrated. This night she was in a different space.

"You know what you say in your manuscript about God not being in control, that God doesn't cause the things that happen to us. How does that fit with all those things in the Bible, like Proverbs where it says 'God directs our paths' and all?"

Karen and I often talked about the Bible. We discussed her question on several occasions. She wanted to review the concept of progressive "revelation" or "understanding"—the idea that what the Bible teaches about God is presented on a long continuum with various points of significant breakthrough in new and ongoing awareness.

The Bible is the true and inspired[8] written record of God's self-revelation in and throughout human experience. But many find it difficult to see the Bible as an inspired record of a progressive revelation and understanding about who God is and how God relates to humanity. We use the term "word of God" freely in the contemporary church to refer to the Bible. The common usage of the biblical term has become synonymous with the Bible, but no writer in the Bible ever claimed that these words were written as God dictated them. This is an unfortunate and inaccurate concept. It is easy to forget that the literal meaning of the words in the Bible have no power in themselves. Rather it is the experience one has with the living God.

Jesus noted that of themselves there is no salvation in the Scriptures. Jesus challenged the tendency to sanctify the Bible, as common in his day as it is today. Speaking to a group of religious leaders, Jesus said, "You search the Scriptures because you think in them you have eternal life" (Jn 5:39).

Dr. Wayne Rollins, professor of religious studies and director of the Ecumenical Institute at Assumption College in Massachusetts, has a powerful way to express this. Rollins notes that the group of religious leaders Jesus was speaking to

> were under the impression that the bottom line in Scripture was the text itself. For Jesus, the bottom line was the presence of the living God, to whom the text unerringly points and to whom it constantly seeks to draw our attention. As a contemporary Benedictine comments, 'We do not stop at the word God speaks, but at the God who speaks in his word.'

> ...*the Bible is not the words of God, but the Word of God.* Historical criticism has impressed us indelibly with the truth that the words of Scripture are the words of their scriptural authors. It is through *their words,* and through their grammar and syntax, that *the Word* is refracted.... When John speaks of the Word becoming flesh or when Paul prays for a door to be opened for the Word, neither has in mind the 773,692 *words* of the English Bible, not to mention the corresponding number in the Hebrew and Greek originals.... In every instance, the phrase [the Word of God] refers to the power and presence of God at work in his world, not to words about him.[9]

There was a tone of urgency in Karen's voice as she continued:

> *"You know, what you were saying about how God is involved in our lives, but not in control? I know what you say in your book...that you believe God does not cause the things that happen to us. But how does that fit with some things you read in the Bible?"*

The answer to her confusion lay in the concept of a progressive understanding of God as opposed to an understanding historically fixed at a point in ancient times. I answered with a story.

> *"Karen, there is a story going around about a man who almost killed one of his children. According to the newspaper account, he was a religious man who worshiped regularly and*

seemed to live a fairly faithful and godly life. People in his racially mixed neighborhood liked and respected him. This man was praying one day when he began to hear God telling him to take one of his children—a favorite son— and kill him. This man was actually convinced that he would please God if he killed his son as a sacrifice. This man believed that God would bless him for his faithfulness.

I paused. Karen was becoming a bit suspicious of my news story. She listened attentively, but there was a wary look on her face.

"Karen, if you had read that story on the front page of this morning's newspaper, what would you have thought?"
"He was crazy. Did he kill him? You're not talking about something that really happened, are you? If you are, he's insane and needs to be locked up! Anyone who would believe God is telling him to kill his own child is nuts."
"I agree. But Karen, it did happen and the man was not crazy. Do you remember the story of Abraham and Isaac?"
"Yeah. But that was different, I mean...."

Karen couldn't complete her sentence. She stopped and listened to her own words.

"Karen, that is what I mean when I say the Bible is true. But much of the truth was still in process when it was given. Abraham really believed that the God he worshiped was the kind of God who would ask a man to kill his own son. You and I know that is not true. Our God is not a pagan mythological deity who is as cruel as the creatures he created. Did God change? Was there a time when God really found pleasure in people killing each other as acts of faithfulness and worship? I think not. God has not changed. But, thank God, our understanding of who and what God is has continued to change."
"Then maybe I've been wrong about God." Karen paused.
"I mean.... Oh, I'm not sure what I mean. Maybe I've just been wrong about some things."

The biblical story of Abraham and Isaac is a classic example of the development of humanity's understanding of God. Abraham's belief that God would actually demand that a father butcher his son like a sacrificial lamb and burn him as an offering would sound reasonable in his day. Such an act would bring God's favor upon him. It was consistent with the theological and psychological knowledge available at that point in history. Archaeological evidence indicates that human sacrifice was a fairly universal practice at various times and places in history. Several thousand years later this was interpreted as a test of Abraham's faith and commitment to God. But it is a moot point. This argument is of no consequence since Abraham did not know God was only testing him. Abraham understood Yahweh as a God who would demand that a man kill his son as an act of righteousness.

Abraham was a man of great faith, but his understanding of God was limited. It was, in fact, primitive when compared with the teachings of Jesus and early Christian understanding of the character of God. It is obvious that Abraham thought God wanted him to do something which is contrary to the nature of God as revealed later in the Bible.

In studying the Bible, it seems obvious that Israel often misinterpreted God's interactions in their lives. Their defeat or their victory was considered evidence of God's presence. Numerous factors determined the outcome of their battles. At times, they lost when they should have won. At other times they won when they should have lost. Winning or losing is never the test for proving God's presence. The prophets challenged Israel to do good so that God might be with them. But the prophets were coming to understand a greater truth in that they were called to higher levels of love and mercy and justice because God was with them. God was with Israel in all of their experiences, who they were, and how they lived with their victories and their defeats. The same was true about Israel's enemies. We may try to make things work out our way but we cannot get God to be gracious to the good and ungracious to the bad.

Every time I entered the boxing ring, I wanted God to be on my side and, like Israel did before a battle, I prayed before every boxing match that God would make me the winner. If I trained hard and prayed hard and was good, then God would be on my side. I can understand a child's believing that logic. But as the Apostle Paul said (1 Cor 13:11), when we become an adult we need to put away thinking like a child. It is interesting that Paul says this following the great description of mature love. These are words about the very core of God's nature: love. These are words that challenge us to live the kind of love that would make battles unnecessary, and the thought that God's presence and favor is with those who win battles sheer foolishness.

I was a kid; I wanted God to be on my side just as the youthful Israel did when it faced the enemy. But God was on my opponent's side—and on my side. No doubt God had little interest in who won the boxing match, but God was interested in each of us and how we lived out our victories and our defeats in the ring and outside the ring. God was in each one luring us to a better meaning in life.

Ira Lolli's interest in me did not depend on whether I won or lost. He was in my corner, but he was only human, and his graciousness was flawed because he could not be in my opponent's corner. He wanted me to win, but he didn't want either of us to be hurt. He even cheered for my opponent when he was fighting someone else. But Ira, of course, wanted me to defeat all of my opponents not because I was on the side of good and right and my opponent was not, but because I was one of his boys.

We have the idea that there is always a right side and a wrong side in a disagreement, with God always favoring those who are right. This makes it easier at times for us to convince ourselves that God is in our corner.

Sarah's answer means that God lives in each human being, that God enters into the created order of life and is in every evolving and developing aspect of the universe in general, but particularly in the human person. God is in every single human being, experiencing that person's struggles and joy. God is much more a part of human experience than many traditional thinkers believe. Some of the Augustinian persuasion as well as others who follow the thinking of the reformers place the emphasis on God as being completed perfection beyond any new experience, fixed and removed from sinful humanity. This thinking places God totally apart from us. Thus, when we are bad or when bad things happen to us, God is not there. God cannot tolerate evil and moves away from the presence of evil. We experience this kind of God only when we are good or repentant. I believe the life of Jesus says something uniquely different and quite the opposite about who and what God is. The life of Jesus makes a profound statement about our everyday life situations. God does not run away when we are in trouble nor does God turn away when we sin; God stays in the ring with us.

God constantly urges and invites each person to the highest good available in every situation. But, bound by divine choice, God does not have control over the choice a person makes. God is powerless to make people choose the good. That was God's choice from the beginning of creation. God entered into all human experience and does not withdraw from any human event—good or bad.

As the session closed that night, Karen thought long and hard. Then, looking at the photos of herself as a child, she said,

"She was not bad. What her father said was not true. He often told her, 'You are bad. It would not hurt so much if you were not so little. You are small for six...that is why it hurts. Stop crying right now! You are bad!'"

"She didn't deserve it." Karen continued, "They did not deserve to get away with it. They blamed her, and they got away with it!"

Karen reached a major milestone in her journey. I dreaded facing the next one.

NOTES

1. Gustavo Gutierrez, *Job: God-Talk and the Suffering of the Innocent* (Maryknoll, New York: Orbis Books, 1987), p. xi.

2. *The Analytical Greek Lexicon* (Grand Rapids, Michigan: Zondervan, 1978), p. 165.

3. Lewis S. Ford, *The Lure of God* (Philadelphia: Fortress Press, 1978), pp. 130ff.

4. Charles Colson, "Inclusive Anguish," *Christianity Today*, December 8, 1988, p. 80.

5. J. B. Phillips, *Your God Is Too Small* (New York: Macmillan Publishing Co., 1987).

6. Howard Clinebell, "Growing Through Loss." Video, United Methodist Communications, Interfaith Media Center, Claremont, California.

7. Flora Rheta Schreiber, *Sybil* (New York: Warner Books, Inc., 1974).

8. In 2 Timothy 3:16, Paul indicates that Scripture in his time was understood to be the Torah and possibly other portions of what Christian tradition has called the Old Testament. He says that Scripture is inspired. He does not explain how it comes to be inspired, but says it is useful for teaching and guiding. He does not claim that Scripture teaches infallible historical or sci-

entific facts; he merely asserts that it is inspired truth about God and how we are to live in relation to God.

9. Wayne G. Rollins, *Jung and the Bible* (Louisville, Kentucky: Westminster/John Knox Press, 1983), p. 95.

CHAPTER SIX

AN INCREDIBLE DEDUCTION:
God Is With Us, In Us

Because I don't know Thomas's father, I can't be sure whether his behavior ever haunted him. Personally, I find it hard to talk about perpetrators of incest. I experience anger toward them much sooner than their victim does. I could no longer evade the distasteful thought that lingered in the shadows of my mind. What if Thomas's father asked the same questions of me?

> *"Horace, where was God when I was raping my son? Why didn't God do something? Where was he? Why didn't he stop me?"*

This is the most difficult and incomprehensible part of the mystery of God's grace. If God is in me when I lose, if God was in Thomas and Karen when they were raped, if God is empowering us to endure and offering us the help to make our lives worth living despite what happens to us, where is God? And what is God doing in relation to the person who is the abuser?

Some readers may want to move on to the next chapters which emphasize how God's grace offers hope to deal with the scars that evil encounters inflict. However, if you are open to considering a radical idea of grace, let's explore beyond the traditional and comfortable understanding of God and consider some of Jesus' most mysterious words.

Let me clarify an earlier statement about the illusion that God is only in *our* corner. Martin Niemoller spoke prophetically on this during an address to the 1952 World Conference of Christian Youth in

Kottayam, South India. In his talk about his rediscovery of the gospel following eight years of imprisonment in a German concentration camp, Niemoller said, "It has been the greatest lesson of my life to see that God is not the enemy of my enemies; God is not even the enemy of his own enemies."

A beautiful statement in the ancient Hebrew Seder expresses this very idea in the section which recounts Israel's escape from Egypt. The reader tells of the Israelites' rejoicing as they see their Egyptian pursuers destroyed in the waters of the Red Sea. It is obvious that Israel sees the death of the Egyptian army as a miraculous divine intervention on their behalf. God is on their side. God has worked a miracle to save them. They were good and God was blessing them. Their enemies were bad and God was punishing them. Whether or not God forced the change of the natural order to create a giant tidal wave is an important issue in hermeneutics and exegesis. Of greater significance is that Israel thought of themselves as God's only children. Their enemies were not God's children. Centuries later the fuller canon of the Bible makes it clear that the Egyptians were also God's children, that peoples of all nations are the focus of God's love. This concept has been a part of the Seder for centuries. During the service, the father reads the description of the Ten Plagues, followed with readings by the eldest son and the mother of the family.

> *Son:* The Lord caused the waters to be divided and the Israelites passed over safely; then the waters closed on the Egyptians, with their chariots of war. Thus the children of Israel became free.

> *Mother:* But as with the ten plagues, there is a story in our tradition about the Egyptians who drowned. When the Israelites crossed over safely, the angels in heaven began to sing in praise of God. But God looked down on the waters closing over the Egyptians and cried, "How can you sing when my children are drowning?"

It is hard to believe that God is as interested in our enemies as in us and is present with our enemies even when we are right and they are wrong. God is gracious to the good and the bad. Jesus said that God "…is kind to the ungrateful and the evil" (Lk 6:35). He reminds us that "the sun shines on the just and the unjust" (Mt 5:45). So do chicken pox, cancer, and social security benefits, on people born in Africa, or Alaska, or Arkansas.

God is God to our enemies and to us. That is, God's attitude is the same toward us and toward our enemies—individually and collectively.

Consider now some of Jesus' most mysterious words. The twenty-fifth chapter of Matthew records one of Jesus' warnings about the connections humans have with one another and with God. He clarifies how delicate and interwoven relationships are. Like many people today, Jesus' disciples were concerned about the future of the nation of Israel and the end of the created order. In response to their questions about these issues, Jesus challenged them to look at present relations, not at future times or events. Jesus seems to have had a simple motto: Take good care of today and tomorrow will be all right.

Jesus' words in this chapter are difficult to sort out. He tells a story about a king who judges the good and the bad people in his kingdom. It is difficult to determine when Jesus is speaking of the nation of Israel and the Roman empire, when he is speaking of the end of the created order, when he is speaking metaphorically or allegorically, and when, if at all, he is speaking literally.

These points make interesting material for discussion. There is little argument with the fact that we are to live by grace. Jesus warned of the danger of living unaware of God's grace and presence. In his story of judgment, Jesus focuses on one central factor that separates the "goats" and the "sheep," the good and the bad. The difference is the way they treat each other.

To those he called good the king said, "...I was hungry and you fed me; I was thirsty and you gave me water, I was a stranger and you invited me into your homes, naked and you clothed me."

To those he called bad the king said, "...I was hungry and you wouldn't feed me; thirsty, and you wouldn't give me anything to drink; a stranger, and you refused me hospitality; naked, and you wouldn't clothe me; sick and in prison, and you didn't visit me."

Both groups insist that they do not know what the king is talking about. Each asks, "When did we do that to you?" The king replies, "When you did it to these my brothers you were doing it to me, and when you refused to help the least of these my brothers, you were refusing to help me."

The conclusions are obvious. Jesus is saying that the way you and I treat each other is inseparable from God. When I am good to you, I am good to God who is alive in both of us. God experiences what is going on in me as I relate to you. At the same time, God participates in your experience of how I treat you. When I am mean to you, I am mean to God. Whatever I do to you I do to God! We can forget our childish fears that God might find out what we do and hold us accountable. God doesn't find out. God knows it and experiences it fully since God is part of who we are and what we do.

When we abuse others—friend or foe—God chooses to take their experience into the divine nature. This is a dreadful thought. My choices compel God to be a victim of my oppression. Because God is committed to a choice not to control and dominate human experience, God cannot arbitrarily stop any action based on human choice. What I do, then, I do to God. What happens to you happens to God.

But there is a greater and more formidable side to this. When I choose to do evil, I also compel God to endure my experience as a perpetrator. God endures what I feel and think as I perform any act of evil.

When Richard Speck chose to kill eight nurses in Chicago, God was there, calling to him, "Don't do it!" God did not abandon the eight women. God felt their horror and pain, their death. In those moments of life and death God was in them, trying to comfort them, urging them to face death with hope. God could not run from their experience.

Likewise, God could not abandon Richard Speck even in that hideous moment. God's grace was there urging him to stop, pleading with him to be merciful, just, and loving.

This compounds the heinousness of all evil acts. The wrong one does to another is grotesque. A Nazi kicks a chair from under the feet of an innocent child. In doing that he overrules the grace of God within himself and defiles the very image of God within himself. In that action he exposes God to the sick emotional acceleration and the muted revolution of a seared conscience that explodes within him. If there is a judgment—be it present or future—how great is the judgment on one who plunders the grace of God by exposing God to the experience of perverted evil! It is insane for anyone to ignore God's grace, to refuse grace, but how grossly evil it is to willfully desecrate it.

Shug Avery, the free-spirited singer in Alice Walker's novel, *The Color Purple,* is a good example of how common folk who live close to the good and bad in all of us, quite often have an uncanny awareness of the presence of God's grace. Shug's crude words aren't likely to be heard in polite society or from a pulpit. But no one spoke more graphically about the absurdity of ignoring the grace of God that is all about us and in us.

In the film of the same title, Shug and her friend Celie walk through a field of purple bluebonnets, literally adrift in a sea of magnificent purple that swirls in the breeze. Shug waves to the flowers and comments about God's presence revealed in the purple flowers.

> Here's the thing, say Shug. The thing I believe. God is inside you and inside everybody else. You come into the world with God. But only them that search for it inside find it. And sometimes it just manifest itself even if you not looking, or don't know what you looking for. Trouble do it for most folks, I think....
> It? I ast.
> Yeah, It. God ain't a he or a she, but a It.
> But what do it look like? I ast.
> Don't look like nothing, she say. It ain't a picture show. It ain't something you can look at apart from anything else, including yourself. I believe God is everything, say Shug. Everything that is or ever was or ever will be. And when you can feel that, and be happy to feel that, you've found It.
> I think it pisses God off if you walk by the color purple in a field somewhere and don't notice it.[1]

We are participants in the grace of God whether we like it or not. Walker draws on her understanding of the symbolic meaning of the color purple in the Christian church—the symbol of grace. Her story is impregnated with the theme of grace. Her characters live and sin, suffer, rejoice and die in a world stained with purple—God's grace.

At times, Shug had the eyes of Jesus. She saw God's grace everywhere in everything—even amid sin and shame and abuse. In one scene in the movie, Shug is in a tavern when she hears singing in an adjacent church. Her minister father is leading the congregation in a hymn. Shug begins to sing the hymn and leads a crowd of people from the local tavern right into the midst of the church service. As she faces her staunch preacher father, she cries, "See, Daddy, sinners have soul too!" Father and daughter embrace in the grace of mutual forgiveness.

Grace speaks to the spirit. It is from the spirit that grace acts. We cannot escape God's grace. God is powerless to control our lives. We, in turn, are powerless to control God's grace. But in the midst of such powerlessness resides the greatest power in the universe: the power of grace, the unmerited, undeserved good intentions of one toward another. Here is the new ethic for human relationships: the grace of God—new not in the sense it has never been, but new as one becomes aware. Like the purple of the wild flowers in the open field, we have ignored the magnitude of grace too long in the fields of human relationships. Here is a different motivation for treating other human beings graciously, the true ethic for the godly life. When we are gracious to others, we extend God to another and encounter God in the other. When others wrong us, we are not alone; God endures it with us. This is motivation for gracious living. When we are tempted or feel driven to wrong others, God is there in us, urging us to refrain from evil, to do the good, to be gracious. When we overrule that urge and ignore that invitation, it is a grievous, sinful deed. For in any act of evil, we discredit the presence of the living God within us and within the other.

Elizabeth Barrett Browning speaks of Shug's insight more poetically as she reflects on Moses' experience with the burning bush in Exodus, chapter three.

> Earth's crammed with heaven.
> And every common bush afire with God;
> But only he who sees takes off his shoes;
> The rest sit round it and pluck blackberries.[2]

In Luke's gospel (23:34) Jesus says something interesting about those who were crucifying him: "Father, forgive them for they do not know what they are doing." We usually think Jesus was referring to those accusing him, those who did not realize who he was and what they were doing to him—God incarnate, innocent of the charges brought against him. Could Jesus be saying they did not understand they were crucifying God in a unique human being? Jesus was a specific manifestation of God's grace extended to the world. In him, God was offering a clear example and model of what it is like to live in full harmony with oneself, with God, with one's sisters and brothers of the human race. Those who spurned him and killed him were ignorant and unaware of this. They truly did not know what they were doing. If we take God's presence in us—incarnate—seriously,

Jesus' words are magnified a hundred times. The meaning of the incarnation is that God was in Jesus, living and experiencing in human flesh what it is like to be human. Jesus says that what is true of him is also true of us—God is incarnate in all of us. When we abuse and mistreat one another, we truly do not know what we are doing.

In the life, death, and resurrection of Jesus of Nazareth, God has broken into human experience in a unique way. What we see in Jesus is God's self-sacrifice in a human medium as an ultimate act of grace extended to humanity. But God is not a pagan god who wants human sacrifice to appease his wrath. God is the ultimate eternal being who, Hosea said, "is not a man" (11:9), who Moses called "the eternal present I AM" (Ex 3:14), who Jesus said is "spirit" (Jn 4:24), and who Paul said is that which actually holds all things together (Acts 17). In modern parlance, God is the personal, living power and dynamic life force of all that is. God is the personification of what is called, in the limits of human language, grace and love. In Jesus, God's grace and love are demonstrated concretely and uniquely. In the crucifixion we see the truth of Ira Lolli's words immortalized for all eternity: "You are going to a cross to die, but you do not have to stop living." That truth is universal and eternal. God is with us and in us, calling us to grace and graciousness in all of life. A few lines of a poem I recall from my youth speak to this. I do not remember the name of the speaker at the banquet for the Jones Elementary School football team in Hot Springs, Arkansas. That was forty-four years ago and I was only twelve. But I remember the last lines of the poem he quoted that night.

> When the great Scorer comes to write beside your name,
> It counts not that you won or lost,
> But how you played the game.

That's what grace is about. God is with us in life's game to help us play it well. At the conclusion of chapter four, I remarked that "being God" is risky business. If God lives by the rules of the divine creative process and remains powerless to overrule human free will and choice, we are all at risk of things going awry. There are no guarantees in this world that things will always turn out for the best. Yet, paradoxically, it is out of God's self-imposed powerlessness that God is able to enter into our experience and actually be with us. This is the meaning of grace. God is with us.

Equally paradoxical is the fact that we are powerless to affect God's grace. We can accept it, reject it, even ignore it—but we cannot change it or stop it from existing. We cannot make it different or less than it is. God's grace is there even for those who are unaware of it. I recall from a science class an old puzzle that asked, "If no one is in the forest when a tree falls is there still sound?" Does sound exist if no one hears the vibrations?

God's grace is with us if we "hear" it—recognize it—or not. What does that really mean for a Thomas or a Karen or for people like you and me? What is the bottom line? What does God's grace, God's indwelling presence mean when things are very bad?

Lewis B. Smedes expressed this question well in a small book entitled *How Can It Be All Right When Everything Is All Wrong?* I know well the people Smedes talks about in his chapter titled "Gift of Grace." It happened over thirty years ago. Jackie was one of the first patients I sat with as she lay near death. A young woman in her early thirties, Jackie had given birth to a baby girl only weeks before and she was dying of a brain tumor. She and Ed had five other children and we feared she would die before this birth. As we talked that last time, she said those strange words which I have heard again and again from dying patients: "It's all right." She was sad. She had so much to live for. There was so much yet to do in life, so many who needed her. She was dying, but somehow she could say, "It's all right."

It was 5 a.m. when Ed and I walked out of the hospital. He was a strong, handsome man but his powerful shoulders shook with grief as he sobbed, "What am I going to do without her? I love her so much. What will the kids do without her? Why did she have to die? I don't understand. We need her!" Ed and Jackie had everything to live for. They were good people, faithful Christian church members. Ed taught the men's Bible class each Sunday and Jackie sang in the choir. Ed saw nothing right about Jackie's death. It was wrong—all wrong!

Good and kind, loving young mothers should not die. Good, loving fathers should not be left alone with six children to raise. Jackie's last statement raises the greatest metaphor of life's deepest question: "How can anyone really believe it is all right when everything is hopelessly wrong?"

That is the ultimate question for the Thomases and the Karens and for all of us. When we are knocked down, where do we get the strength to get on our feet again? When our knees are so wobbly we can hardly walk, when we are dazed and our minds are spinning with lightheadedness, where do we find the courage to take another step? When we are devastated by pain, betrayal, and death, how can we find the courage to go on living? Where do people find the courage to go on living? Where do people find the wherewithal to believe that life can be all right when everything in their world is all wrong?

Grace! Pete said, *"Hal, it is grace, all grace!"*

Smedes reminds us that some of the most commonplace things in life come alive as uncommon truth when they come at the right moment. He notes: "What a trite comfort—'It's all right.' A boy strikes out in a Little League game: 'It's all right,' says the coach. A guest spills coffee on a clean tablecloth: 'It's all right,' says the hostess. A baby cries in the night: 'It's all right,' says the mother...."[3]

But we are not talking about tablecloths and Little League ball games. We're talking about the very essence of life and death— tragedy and violence and evil actions. In this context the commonplace becomes either profound or profane—self-deceiving death or self-empowering life!

In 1967 Thomas A. Harris wrote a book called *I'm OK—You're OK*. In this book he sets out the concepts of transactional analysis. His thesis centers on four basic positions or mindsets that people live out in human relationships. They are:

- I'm not OK; you're OK.
- I'm not OK; You're not OK.
- I'm OK; you're not OK.
- I'm OK; you're OK.[4]

Harris sees the last mindset as the position for healthy and positive relations. Some religious critics retorted sarcastically to his idea, "I'm OK, you're OK? Who says so?" That is a valid question with a real answer. The answer is "Grace says so!" I'm OK, you're OK! No matter what happens to you or what you have done, grace says it can be all right, you can be all right. That is what God and grace are all about.

How does God's grace work? It doesn't make everything right or whole or cured. Grace does not mean that God changes things but that God is with us whether things change or not. Grace's goal is to show us that we are all right. It is right for us to live even when others say we don't deserve to live. Grace is the voice of God telling us that it is all right—we are right—to go on breathing and feeling and hoping even while everything in the world around us is chaotic. Even when we have failed or sinned grievously and are judged by self or others to deserve no grace, it is OK. Grace is God present and alive—alive in our deepest fears and hurts—urging us to turn defeat into victory, disgrace into honor, fear into faith, evil into good, hate into love, and even death into life. Grace is the power to see life as it is, admit it is wrong at times—all wrong—and still know in the core of our being that it is all right.

There is hope. There is grace.

> It is the nature of God's grace
> to make all things
> all right.

> An excuse for doing wrong?
> A license for sinning?
> No. To the contrary.
> A healthy compassion
> for doing good!

NOTES

1. Alice Walker, *The Color Purple* (New York: Washington Square Press, 1983), pp. 177-78.
2. Elizabeth Barrett Browning, "Aurora Leigh," Bk. VII, line 820.
3. Lewis B. Smedes, *How Can It Be All Right When Everything Is All Wrong?* (San Francisco: Harper & Row Publishers, 1982), p. 1.
4. Thomas A. Harris, *I'm OK, You're OK* (New York: Harper and Row, Publishers, 1969), p. 43.

CHAPTER SEVEN

THE SECRET:
Six Times Down; Seven Times Up

Grace. Hope. "It's all right. You're all right." Karen understood those words, but to claim them for herself was difficult. It is hard to change our view of life. We are vested in perceptions that justify our view of life. We resist efforts to change them, even when they are distorted and cause us pain.

Believe it or not, there is a secret to living and to overcoming the bad and tragic things that happen to us. I learned this secret as a kid but didn't realize it until much later in life. I became particularly aware of it when I observed the lives of people like Thomas, Sarah, and Karen. It is the secret that enables people to survive the traumas and losses of life. Many, though, who survive by this secret never really understand it. That is the difference between surviving and living. Those who just survive often hope life might be different and even think it might be different for others. In reality, they use the secret but are unaware of it. Those who do become aware of the secret not only survive but also achieve some degree of living in a positive stance.

What is the secret? I have talked about it many times in the pages you've read. Some readers may have discovered it in chapter two, while others did so much later. If you feel you still have missed it, don't be concerned. There is time. Karen discovered it finally in the life of Job.

To talk of God, tragedy, or evil without mentioning the Book of Job, the divinely inspired biblical novel, is like studying literature without reading Shakespeare. On the one hand, the Book of Job is about theology; it addresses the basis of the relationship btween God and human beings. It clearly states that God's grace is not conditioned by or dependent upon human merit. It dismisses the faulty theology of prosperity and merit. On the other hand, it gives a powerful and practical model of the way a person can overcome bad things in life. Job was a man who lived in a world like ours, a world filled with good things and bad things that did not always turn out for the best. Job discovered the secret to survive. Unfair and tragic events stripped him of his health and fortune but he found a way to go on living with meaning and purpose.

The Bible story presents Job as a good and just man who had faith in God and lived that faith. Job and his friends saw his blessings as evidence of God's grace. However, some contended that God was gracious toward Job only because he was a good man. God's grace is conditional.

Others claimed that Job's faith was also conditional and that he was faithful only because God was gracious. Each teeters on the balance of their respective self-serving personal interest. At the heart of this view of grace is a system of cause and effect: a retribution theology. It is a grace that is based on and controlled by earned or deserved merit. At the center of this contention, the Satan character voices the claim that humanity cannot be trusted and casts doubt on God's wisdom in trusting the actions of men and women. The Satan[1] claims that the motives of men are purely selfish.

In the prologue to the Book of Job, the Satan induces God to put Job (humanity) to the test. The plot is set. To understand the underlying plot of the novel, it is important to remember that to the Hebrew of Job's day there were three major signs of God's pleasure with a man; namely, the number of children he had (especially male children), the size of his herds, and his health. The high value placed on the birth of a son was proof of God's pleasure and evidenced in the common practice of Hebrew men fathering children by multiple wives and concubines (Gn 16:3; 25:6). As the inspired writer weaves the story, we discover that in spite of his goodness, Job loses his sons and daughters, his wealth, and his health. Only his wife survives. This tragic development is a true-to-life drama about living in a world where conditions are far from favorable.

Archibald MacLeish has beautifully shown the universality of the ancient biblical story in his contemporary poetic play, *J.B.* The play is based on the Book of Job. It opens on a stage in the corner of a large circus tent. As the play begins, two hawkers enter: Mr. Zuss with his balloons and Nickles who sells popcorn. Mr. Zuss and Nickles sit atop a lighted platform that overlooks a dimly lighted stage. Their talk about balloons and popcorn gradually merges into a verbal struggle about the meaning of life, the relationship between God and human beings, and the concept of good and evil. As the plot develops, Mr. Zuss and Nickles use the masks of Greek actors and take on the biblical roles of God and the Satan. In time, the family and friends of a character named J.B. play out their discussion on the stage below. Early in the play, Nickles sings a rhyme that challenges the core of logic many give to explain evil and suffering.

> *Nickles:* I heard upon his dry dung heap
> That man cry out who cannot sleep:
> "If God is God He is not good,
> If God is good He is not God;
> Take the even, take the odd,
> I would not sleep here if I could
> Except for the little green leaves in the wood
> And the wind on the water...."[2]

Mr. Zuss intones that someone is playing Job, and Nickles comments that there are thousands, millions of Jobs in the world.

> *Nickles:* Millions and millions of mankind
> Burned, crushed, broken, mutilated,
> Slaughtered, and for what? For thinking!
> For walking around the world in the wrong
> Skin, the wrong-shaped noses, eyelids:
> Sleeping the wrong night wrong city—
> London, Dresden, Hiroshima.
> There never could have been so many
> Suffered more for less....
>
> Job is everywhere we go,
> His children dead, his work for nothing,
> Counting his losses, scraping his boils,
> Discussing himself with his friends and physicians,
> Questioning everything—the time, the stars,
> His own soul, God's providence....[3]

Mr. Zuss and Nickles continue their discussion of the plight of humankind. The lights dim and each puts on his actor's mask. From behind the god-mask, Mr. Zuss speaks to Nickles:

> Hast thou considered my servant Job
> That there is none like him on the earth
> A perfect and an upright man...[4]

The platform lights dim and a brilliant light below floods a table where J.B., his wife, and their five children are seated. It is Thanksgiving. J.B. offers a prayer.

A chorus of "Amens" is heard from the children, eager to taste the large succulent bird. The dinner conversation centers on thankfulness. J.B. plays the role of a responsible parent concerned about his children's understanding of the deeper meaning of Thanksgiving.

As the play progresses, Nickles becomes cynical about J.B.'s thankfulness. He points out to Mr. Zuss that it is easy to be thankful when your stomach is full. Mr. Zuss assures Nickles that J.B. is grateful for what he has. Then from behind the Satan mask Nickles counters:

> Bought and paid for like a waiter's smirk!
> You know what talks when that man's talking?
> All that gravy on his plate—
> His cash—his pretty wife—his children!
> Lift the lot of them, he'd sing
> Another canticle to different music.[5]

The play, following the biblical version, continues. J.B.'s children are killed. One is raped and murdered; one is crushed to death by falling stones; one is killed because of an officer's stupidity on a battlefield; two are killed by a drunken teenager. The devastation continues. J.B. is bankrupt, his wife leaves him, and his health begins to fail. Finally, destitute, sick and alone, J.B. sits in rags amid the shambles of his once well-appointed home. He sits in silence. Then he speaks violently the ancient words of Job, "Though he slay me, yet will I trust in him...." J.B. as Job maintains his innocence before God.

In MacLeish's play, J.B. maintains, as Job did, that he is innocent of wrongdoing and regardless of what happens to him he will not give up his trust in God. J.B. and Job hold on tenaciously to faith and integrity. Others accuse them of being unscrupulous, saying they were good men only because of God's blessings. Their character was for sale. Even when stripped unjustly of their blessings, they resolutely refuse to "cop a plea." In the eyes of their peers they were guilty. But they would not plead guilty to deserving the bad things in their lives even in the hope of a lesser sentence. They would take their chances in the court of the Almighty. They would rather suffer and die clinging to the truth—they do not deserve this—than to compromise their integrity to gain a reprieve.

In the biblical novel and in the contemporary play, two major themes play in harmony. One is the limit of human and divine control. The other is the basis of human and divine relationship. These are the themes of chapters four and five in this book (the mystery of God's powerlessness before human free will and the demand of humanity's powerlessness before God's grace). Faith and integrity are at the core of both themes.

The demand of integrity is that God and humanity cannot violate each other's being—who and what each is. God will not—God cannot—force us to be good. We cannot—will not—force God to be ungracious. This is the incomprehensible reality of God's grace. We can do nothing to create it, alter it, or in any way control or manipulate it. We are powerless before God's grace. God is gracious to us whether we like it or not, accept it or not. Here God and humanity ultimately meet in the divinely ordained mutual powerlessness of respectful integrity.

In the mystery of grace, God and humanity are compelled to rely, in faith, one on the other. In the eons of divine forethought God conceived grace as the ultimate framework for the relationship between humanity and divinity. This is the hope and the power of human life: God and man, God and woman in a living relationship which fills life with meaning and purpose. It is a relationship grounded in mutual integrity and lived out in mutual faith and trust.

Job and J.B. hold resolutely and uncompromisingly to their faith and their integrity. Regardless of what happens to them, neither Job nor J.B. give up who they are. Neither is able to give up his faith in God. To Job and J.B., faith in God is synonymous with faith in life itself. Readers of these authors will discover this is likewise true of God. God will not compromise the divine integrity nor will God relinquish the divine faith in humanity's capacity to live by faith under all circumstances. God is betting on Job's faith. God can trust Job to live by faith even when he finds life paradoxical, incomprehensible, unfair, and at times, overrun by evil.

These are the secrets of the Job character: integrity and faith. With faith and integrity, Job and J.B. can endure anything and will survive. The turning point in both dramas occurs when the heroes realize that their complaints are accurate: It is not fair. I don't deserve this. The fight was fixed! Their friends are amazed that God allows their complaints while, at the same time, Job and J.B. discover that God accepts their complaints. Life is just that way. It cannot insure fairness. Our heroes discover that life holds more than success and justice. God invites them beyond the unfairness of life. God did not send it or interfere with its coming. God entered into it with them. In the dark night of the soul they began to see the true basis of their relationship with God.

The closing pages of the biblical novel (42:5-6) reveal this awareness. These verses are among the most opaque verses in the Bible, yet they offer an important insight into the way one overcomes life's dirty deals. Job abruptly appears to make a sudden and total reversal of his claim. He does not abandon his insistence that he did nothing to merit the bad things in his life, yet he confesses and repents. What does Job confess? What does he repent? Gutierrez's translation of these verses offers a variant reading on this difficult Hebrew text and helps to answer these questions. Job says:

> "I once knew you only by hearsay,
> now my eyes have seen you,
> therefore I repudiate and repent
> of dust and ashes."[6]

Gutierrez departs from the traditional translation. The key difference is in the words "repent of dust and ashes" as opposed to "repent in dust and ashes." "In" leaves an important question unanswered. What does Job retract? Job does not accept with resignation those things he considers unjust and wrong. He defends his innocence and integrity; he didn't deserve what happened! If Job is repenting in dust and ashes, what is the content of his repentance? What is the object of his repenting? What is he retracting? He does not name it.

According to L. Alonso Schökel and others, the verb "repent" does not have an object.[7] The reader is required to supply an object for "repent" or settle for what Gutierrez terms ineptitude in the phrase. Gutierrez's translation brings out the rich consistency of the verse with greater depth and clarity. As he notes, "The key to the new version is to be found in the meaning of the verb *naham*, which is correctly translated as 'to repent'. ...[h]owever,...when *naham* is used with the preposition '*al* it means 'to change one's mind' or 'to reverse an opinion.' " Thus the text in Job is saying that Job repudiates and abandons—he actually changes his mind about dust and ashes.

The phrase "dust and ashes" relates to Job's groaning and lamentations. It is a vivid picture of Job's condition before he began complaining. Gutierrez states further, "This, then, is the object of the retraction and change of mind of which this key verse speaks." Job rejects the attitude that has been his until that moment. He retracts his prior world view and his attitude toward the way God and humanity relate. Job sees that his attitude and his reaction to all that happened to him is wrong. Job is coming to a new view of life and how things relate. Gutierrez adds:

> The new translation illumines the whole of Job's second response and makes it more coherent. The Hebrew verb *m's*, "reject, repudiate," is no longer left hanging without an object; it refers, as does the verb "repent" (taken in the sense of "change one's mind") to Job's attitude of protest and reproach: "I repudiate dust and ashes." This means that in his final reply what Job is expressing is not contrition but *a renunciation of his lamentation and dejected outlook*....It is this whole outlook that Job says he is now abandoning.[8]

One might even conjecture that Job is saying that his understanding and attitude toward dust and ashes speaks of his humanity itself. He has a new understanding of what it means to be human. The expectations and the guarantees are far different from his earlier thinking. This provides a keen insight into Job's new awareness about his relationship with God. As Gutierrez notes, traditional commentators on Job's confession have seen it as a simple, "I'm sorry—I was wrong." But there is far more to it than that. Life has wronged Job. Bad things happened to him and he wanted to know why. He doesn't get a straight answer. Why do bad things happen? Because that is the way it is in the world of humanity. Although Job's complaints do not change anything, he does discover two life-changing realities: God is with him no matter what happens; Job has the power to choose the meaning he places on what happens to him. Many difficulties remain but Job's horizon is expanded. This is the switch that opens the currents of hope and energy for starting over. The Book of Job concludes on an "they all lived happily ever after" note:

> The Lord restored his wealth and happiness...the Lord blessed Job at the end of his life more than at the beginning. For now he had 14,000 sheep, 6,000 camels, 1,000 oxen, and 1,000 female donkeys. God also gave him seven more sons and three more daughters (42:10-13).

How did all of this come about? How did Job get back to the good life and have his wealth and happiness restored? In fairy tales a princess godmother waves a magic wand. In real life the wave of a mystical wand does not bring about those kinds of miracles. Rather, it is through God's grace lived out in the faith of a human heart, the ingenuity of a human mind, and the sweat of a human brow.

It is interesting that in the biblical novel the Satan does not take Job's wife from him. Why was she spared? Perhaps she was the unnoticed sign of hope, the symbolic doorway to new life. For a time, she was as confused and frustrated with Job as were his friends. She, too, was a victim of the faulty religious thinking of that day. Her view was narrow and limited to a cause and effect mentality. She also offered pious platitudes filled with poor advice. But in the end she is with Job in his rebuilding. She joins him in living again. Symbolically and literally she gives new life to their relationship. The future is birthed in her—seven sons and three daughters. A person of faith, she, too, will risk it all again!

After all their adversities, Job and his wife had great faith. They had another child and Job's herds grew. He got his sons and daughters and herds the second time by once again entering into the relationships of living, loving, and working. Job knew the risk. He knew the world was a place where there were no guarantees, no assurances. Things could go wrong but he chose to try again, to live again. An old folk saying asserts, "Six times down; seven times up— such is life." I have forgotten who coined the phrase. Perhaps it was Job—or was it Mrs. Job?

Things changed for Job only after he had given up—repudiated and repented of his despair over the injustices of life. The only thing that changed was his attitude, his way of thinking about life, himself, and God. He could not change anything that happened to him, but he came to terms with the truth. He could change his response to anything. As did Viktor Frankl, Job discovered that when one loses hold on life and everything familiar is snatched away, what remains is the "last of human freedoms," the ability to "choose one's attitude in a given set of circumstances."[9] This is the hardest step in overcoming the consequences of being wronged, of being sexually abused. This means letting go—of the past and one's illusions about it, of the pain, of the anguish of being robbed of a value which cannot be replaced.

Perhaps this is what prayer is all about, even petitionary prayer—an encounter with God that changes our life. The power and miracle of prayer lie in honesty. It is a time with God and one's self, in the middle of reality, when we discover that the power and miracle do not lie in inducing God to change things. It is a power that does, at times, mysteriously enable us to change things. But more reliably, it is a power that always enables us to change ourselves. The result of Job's prayer was simple but it set off a chain reaction that affected his world.

I studied Karen closely. She was a mixture of child and adult. Childhood memories were uncomfortable topics for her. Consequently, I found it difficult to push her in those areas. Her reports of childhood events were vague. When I pressed for details, the little girl in her wrenched in anguish and would withdraw. At times I felt guilty—almost abusive. I struggled to offer her gentleness and compassion. Often my inner being became enraged at the abuse the child had endured. She was robbed of so much that cut deep into her being. She could never be an undefiled, innocent child. Never! Repeatedly telling her "I'm sorry" could not grant her a reasonably normal and healthy childhood.

Like Job, Karen had every right to complain. What had happened to her was not right; it just was not fair.

The Book of Job closes abruptly and in a matter-of-fact way. Job recovered more than he had lost and lived well until he died. MacLeish's dramatic version gives an insight on the way Job managed to reclaim the good life again.

As the play builds to a climax, Nickles slings the Satan mask into the corner of the lighted platform. He is disgusted as he sees where

things with J.B. are headed. He speaks to Mr. Zuss who has also removed his mask.

Nickles:	Well, that's that!
Mr. Zuss:	That's...that!
Nickles:	So Job gets his in cash. That's generous....
Mr. Zuss:	Gets all he ever had and more... He gets his wife back, and the children... Follow in nature's course.
Nickles:	You're lying.... Wife back! Balls! He wouldn't touch her. He wouldn't take her with a glove! After all that filth and blood and Fury to begin again! ...He can't!...he won't...he wouldn't touch her.
Mr. Zuss:	He does though.
Nickles:	Live his life again?— Not even the most ignorant, obstinate, Stupid or degraded man This filthy planet ever farrowed, Offered the opportunity to live His bodily life twice over, would accept it— Least of all Job.... It can't be borne twice over! Can't be!
Mr. Zuss:	It is though. Time and again it is— Every blessed generation...[10]

Nickles and Mr. Zuss exit. J.B. stands alone on the stage. He hears
a sound. It is Sarah returning home. Unable to cope with J.B.'s rage
and despair, Sarah had left. Her love for J.B. compels her to return.
As they begin to talk, J.B. reminds her she had once told him to curse
God and die. J.B. asks why she had left him alone. Sarah's insight is

revealing. She assures J.B. she loves him, that she had to leave him because she could not help him. He was obsessed with his demand for justice to the point he closed out everyone else around him. He wanted justice. Sarah knew there was no justice. It was not justice J.B. needed; it was faith.

No justice—that is one of the most painful stings of any abuse of children. There is no justice, and those few situations where there is some degree of legal justice, there is only limited satisfaction. Far too many people get away with the abuse they perpetrate on others. Only in the last twenty years have we begun to face the magnitude of the problems of abuse and violence that occur in the American home. Tougher laws and sentencing are becoming more common within the justice system. For many, this legal response is too little and too late.

Karen's experience in the legal system was anything but just. She felt she was in many ways a victim of the system that should have made things right. It is difficult for a child to stand against father, mother, and, on occasion, against an entire family. In Karen's case many family members wouldn't admit the evil they had committed.

Karen found it hard to trust that anyone really believed her. Obviously, there were those who did not believe her. One of Karen's deepest wounds was the constant awareness that no one in her family had "paid for what they did." As with J.B., there was no justice.

"They moved a few weeks ago." Karen had met her sister on a recent business trip. She told her their parents had sold "the old house" and moved.

"They just threw my things away. They didn't even ask if I wanted any of it. It's like I never existed as far as they're concerned. They did it to me, and it doesn't bother them at all."

My stomach tightened as I listened to Karen. So intensely aware of my feelings, I felt I was on an emotional roller coaster; my anger spiked in fleeting fantasies of what Karen's family deserved. Then a sudden sense of sadness engulfed me. No one should suffer so much. It was not the first time I found it difficult to maintain a healthy distance from Karen's experience.

Her voice was cold but brittle. *"They just go on like nothing*

*ever happened. Even Beverly who told me about their moving
and throwing away my stuff doesn't think it was any big deal. It
isn't fair. They did it to me and got away with it scot-free. It
isn't fair."*

The thought that they continued to go on as if nothing ever happened often haunted Karen. Karen had disassociated herself from her
family. A supportive family had legally adopted her and she changed
her name. These steps helped, but there still was no justice. No one
paid for their sin. No one said, "I did it and I'm sorry."

Justice is an ambiguous thing. Most of us are taught from childhood
that when you do wrong you are punished. We say this is only right;
this is justice. Aside from the deterrent aspects, punishing the wrong-
doer does not—cannot—undo the damage to the victim. Just punishment for a wrong can be beneficial and help bring rehabilitation to
the one punished. But it cannot take away from the victim the pain,
suffering, and memory of the experience. If Karen's abusers had gotten just punishment, it would not have changed what had happened.
Perhaps it could have helped her to let go of the pain she experienced.
She was, however, denied even that bit of satisfaction.

I began to understand that this was a reason Karen kept the experience of her abuse alive. She was in a veritable "catch 22." Having been abused repeatedly as a child, she was conditioned to think it
was normal. If it was wrong, it was her fault. Everyone in her family
had gone on with their lives. She seemed to be the only one who remembered what had happened to her.

I cannot fathom how the survivors of Auschwitz and Dachau felt
after their liberation. I once stood outside the fence at Dachau and
tried to imagine myself as a survivor of the torture and death that occurred in that hell hole. An incomprehensible sadness and the urge to
destroy that place swept over me. I had a driving impulse to level every stone and burn every board, to stomp and scatter the ashes of that
place, and to scrub the earth clean where the camps once stood.

Following the end of World War II, many others were surely driv-
en by a desire to eradicate those places of evil from the face of the
planet. Many in the world wanted to forget they ever existed. That is
always the conflict for me. My urge to destroy such places of evil
runs head-on into my determination that the world must not forget
what happened in those places.

The museum of Dachau memorializes those who suffered and

died there in those years of degradation. The exhibit is housed in the only remaining original building. Ironically, rabbis and ministers were confined in those barracks. History tells us they were kept in secret isolation apart from the rest of the prisoners. Pictures of the infamy fill the museum: starved men and women, bodies of dead men and women piled fifteen feet high in trenches that bulldozers had dug, a child on gallows—lifeless and his tongue hanging from the corner of his mouth. The pictures were life size, but there was no life in that place. At the exit of the museum I paused to read a sign, the words of Santayana written in four languages: *"Those who cannot remember the past are condemned to repeat it."*

Something within us will not let places like Auschwitz and Dachau be totally destroyed. Perhaps it is a deep-seated fear they will be forgotten. We cannot allow such places and such deeds to be forgotten. This need to insure that they are not forgotten is so inherent in us that we build monuments to preserve their place in our history.

This was a part of Karen's dilemma. It seemed that as far as her family was concerned, the abuse had never happened. If she let go of the painful memories, the internalized guilt, the degrading behavior, it would say it had never happened. No one would remember.

In a strange way Karen's life was a real monument to what had happened to her. Karen was giving her life to maintain the monument to her personal Auschwitz. This was one reason why the concept of grace was so difficult for her. The idea of forgiveness was intolerable. It was not that Karen's family was beyond forgiveness. They simply refused to acknowledge anything to confess. Thus, where there is no guilt, there can be no forgiveness.

Karen's real need for forgiveness rested in the inappropriate guilt she harbored in her heart. She needed to confess she was accusing herself and holding onto something that was not her fault. But this self-forgiveness was slow in coming. Karen had to hold on to her abuse—and the consequences. If she didn't keep it alive, it would be forgotten—like nothing ever happened.

Karen wanted justice and I could identify with that. It was not right for them to ignore or escape from the reality. How could Karen forgive them when they rejected her and denied her claims? Why should she forgive them? Why? For her own well-being. Forgiveness centers on letting go and getting on with life. That was the problem: getting on with life equaled letting go—a denial that it ever happened!

131

The need for justice is akin to the need to know why. While both are valid concerns, neither one is the final answer to the problem of living since neither addresses the future. One reason the Book of Job moves to a sudden conclusion after endless stanzas of lamentations and arguments with God is that Job finally moved past his demand for justice, giving up his demand for an explanation of what happened. Over ninety percent of the Book of Job and the J.B. play is taken up with questions that have no answers: Why don't things turn out right? Where is justice?

The difficulty with justice and with explanations is that they are rarely obtainable. Job, wanting some justification for his troubles, demanded that God explain why he was suffering. Suppose God did explain. A telegram from the Divine Department of Justice stating that Job's children died honorably in the defense of the Divine honor would be little consolation to the stricken Job. Is Job expected to forget the injustice he and his children experienced because God won the wager with the Satan? No; Job would have found little consolation in a certificate of divine theological justification for his boils and his bankruptcy. The theological and philosophical explanations of the bad things in life offer little help. With or without justice or explanations, the bottom line is: Where do we go from here? How do we move on?

J.B.'s wife was right. We, like J.B. and Job, want justice. But with or without justice we need grace and love—God and each other. In the play's closing dialogue, J.B.'s wife tells him that the hope of the world is not justice. It is love. J.B. is still hurt. He retorts that God does not love; "He just IS." She insists, "But we do." She insists that this is the wonder of life—that people love.

MacLeish chose the play's closing lines well:

> *J.B.:*   …It's too dark to see.
>
> *Sarah:*   Then blow on the coal of the heart, my darling.
>
> *J.B.:*   The coal of the heart…
>
> *Sarah:*   It's all the light now.
>
> Blow on the coal of the heart.
> The candles in churches are out.

The lights have gone out in the sky.
Blow on the coal of the heart
And we'll see by and by...
We'll know...[11]

At that moment the sun rises through the windows. Day is breaking. Sarah and J.B. begin to clean up the mess of broken furniture and debris scattered around their once well-appointed home. As the curtain falls, Sarah and J.B. are at work putting things back together.

Sarah's words point to the clearest evidence that there is a God and how that God relates to us in and through human relations. Sarah reminds J.B. that when tragedy struck unfairly he wanted justice, but his struggle with justice and a reason why did not restore him to meaning or living. There are many people who waste their lives struggling for the wrong things. I am reminded of the challenge of the Serenity Prayer: "God, grant me the serenity to accept what I cannot change, the courage to change what I can, and the wisdom to know the difference." A Don Quixote is an inspiration to all when he sees beauty and good in an abused, deprived barmaid. But he is a foolish tragedy when he duels with a windmill.

Job and J.B. were dueling with windmills, trying to change what they could not change. They remained pathetic legacies of tragedy so long as they sat in justifiable but self-defeating pity or raged in understandable but fruitless demands for explanations and justice. Freedom from the past and the birth of new life came only when they accepted the grace of God available to them in that place, in that moment—in themselves and in their human companions!

MacLeish's Sarah challenged J.B. (as perhaps did Mrs. Job) to look beyond his wounds and demands for justice to his need for love—the hope of life. Sarah is an inspired pragmatist—a true mystic, an angel of hope, a messiah symbol. "There is no justice," she declares. "There is love." J.B.'s understanding of God is still limited; he is still hurt and depressed. He retorts, "He does not love. He IS." J.B. believes in God—God IS! But he does not understand how and where God IS—and what the IS is! As Richard Bach expressed it:

The
original sin is to
Limit the Is.
Don't.[12]

Sarah has insights that J.B. doesn't have. She knows God *IS* because *LOVE IS*. We love, she concludes, and that is the wonder!

That is the wonder! We can love. We can live again. That is the miracle. We can rise above the hells of Auschwitz and rape and abandonment and defeat. As Mr. Zuss says time and time again, in every blessed generation the J.B.s go on trying to live regardless of what happens to them.

Six times down—seven times up!

There is a sense in which it is reasonable to think that a God creating a world is no big deal. It takes little effort for an Almighty to move upon the chaos of a pre-created, disordered nothingness and demand order and relatedness. This would be especially true if that God did all of that simply by divine, superhuman, supernatural demand and force. Such a God would need only to speak or simply think and the world would be! But if that same God with all those same capacities chose to enter into all of that disordered nothingness and invite and urge order and relatedness, purpose and meaning to become, that would be a miracle! A human would never do it that way.

Regardless of how it occurred, not one of us was there to witness the beginning miracle. There is a still greater miracle that we can observe and experience in everyday life. That is God in a man, a woman, a child, moving upon the chaos of an individual life, calling forth purpose, inspiring meaning, and enhancing visions of potential order. That is the ongoing evidence that there is a living God, a God who IS, a God who is with us in all the experiences of life, inviting us, urging us, luring us to possibilities and to new life. It is a new life that comes, not by the wave of a magic wand but by the risk and sweat of faith and grace and hard work.

After reading a draft of these pages, a colleague of mine—a survivor of a personal Auschwitz—wrote the following:

> Internalizing the abuse is "being" the abuse. It requires me to keep the abuse alive, to make a monument so that I don't lose myself. Externalizing the abuse—"something happened to me"—gives me the freedom to make a living monument to the power of resurrection, the power of the defiant spirit.... The human heart, the living God within the human heart, is more powerful than the forces of evil. Life comes out of death....Inside the monument of Dachau there are human hearts

vowing never to allow such evil again.

If I make a monument to the evil...there is no room to change. It is a monument to death. If I make a monument to the power of the God within me to overcome evil, then that monument is life-giving and death-defying. That monument has the power to change and grow and heal.[13]

Victims of abuse often offer their lives as monuments to the evil they endured. They cannot let it be forgotten. Their personal identity is at times inseparable from the abuse. They become what happened to them.

But there is hope.

We can erect new living monuments.

There is a secret.

The secret is: Six times down—seven times up!

NOTES

1. "The Satan" instead of "Satan" because the Hebrew uses *hassatan,* the noun with an article, expressing the function of the character, not his or her proper name.

2. Archibald MacLeish, *J.B.* (Boston: Houghton Mifflin Company, 1958), p. 11.

3. *Ibid.,* pp. 12-13.

4. *Ibid.,* p. 24.

5. *Ibid.,* p. 46.

6. Gustavo Gutierrez, *On Job: God-Talk and the Suffering of the Innocent* (Maryknoll, New York: Orbis Books, 1987), p. 83.

7. L. Alonso Schökel, *Job: Commentario teologico y literario* (Madrid: Christianidad, 1983), p. 503.

8. Gutierrez, *op. cit.,* pp. 86-87.

9. Viktor Frankl, *Man's Search for Meaning* (Boston: Beacon Press, 1963).

10. MacLeish, *op. cit.,* pp. 133, 142-43.

11. *Ibid.,* pp. 152-53

12. Richard Bach, *Illusions: The Adventures of a Reluctant Messiah* (New York: Dell, 1981), p. 128.

13. "Do Not Let Your Servant Vanish," reflections on *Where Is God When Bad Things Happen?* by "Serenity" (the name given her by another victim of abuse). I remain thankful for Serenity's gift.

CHAPTER EIGHT

THE CHOICE:
If You Get Where You're Going, Where Will You Be?

One of the most difficult moments in the life of abused persons is the moment when they confront their responsibilities. They are not responsible for the past, for what others did to them as children. But they are responsible for the present and how they deal with what happened in the past. Although victims of incest and other kinds of abuse have few choices about their past, they do have choices concerning their future.

Alice in Wonderland is a delightful and foolish bit of writing, laced with wisdom that, it seems, only a child or someone over forty can understand. One of my favorite passages is the conversation between Alice and the Cheshire cat.

> "Cheshire-Puss," she began... "Would you tell me, please, which way I ought to go from here?"
> "That depends a good deal on where you want to get to," said the Cat.
> "I don't much care where—" said Alice.
> "Then it doesn't matter which way you go," said the Cat.
> "—so long as I get somewhere," Alice added as an explanation.
> "Oh, you are sure to do that," said the Cat, "if you only walk long enough."[1]

The cat was right. We are always going somewhere and if we keep going where we are headed, we will get there!

The title of the popular movie, "Back to the Future," is a sad but apt description of many victims of abuse. They find their future by going back to the past and reliving its consequences in the present. There is a process common to the healing experience of every victim. As a counselor, I have dealt with many people whom evil or random tragedy has victimized. Every one of them who overcame the trauma worked through two overarching experiences in their journey to healing. Each faced the anguish of a dark night of the soul with its lingering guilts, fears, and "why" questions. Then each braved the challenge of a bright sunrise of the soul with its hope and hard work. The compounding tragedy is that many, wronged in life, remain in the dark nights, and their lives are little more than an endless wandering. It is somewhat tragic that the phrase "dark night of the soul" rolls easily off the tongue while the phrase "bright sunrise of the soul" is awkward to articulate and is unfamiliar to the ear.

In the book of Job, forty of the forty-two chapters dwell on describing Job's "dark night of the soul"—his problems, complaints, and lamentations. These are "why" issues and in these forty chapters Job is mired down in anguish, pain, and confusion. He barely survives. In the last chapter, however, the story takes a sudden, drastic change and within a few verses Job rises above his adversities and begins to get on with life. Suddenly, there is a future. The abrupt change in Job is misleading. The author gives no details about the metamorphosis. But in chapter seven we saw that the explosion of change comes from Job's decision to let go of the injustices and losses of the past. Once again he sees himself as a human being created in the image of God, not a mass of frothing protoplasm devoid of the divine spirit and energy.

The actions Job begins to take give evidence of a new set of questions. Job's verbs become present tense, future-oriented, and active. *What can I do to experience life again? How can I go on?* The answers to these questions usher in a new day for Job. Everyone like Job and J.B. begins at some point to ask why and demand justice. At such times, we may be accused of having a "pity party." Whatever one calls such moments, they are never adequate. They rarely resolve anything and are never necessary to one's moving on.

At times, life appears to be an ongoing dialogue with two basic questions: Why and how? Both have a varied list of expressions; both have a place in the scheme of things. "Why" questions take many forms, centering on what has already occurred. Why are things the way they are? The "how" questions of life pivot about what can be. "Why" tends to explain and gives reasons. "How" points to action and invites engagement with change. Each is valid. Each has a place in dealing with life. However, even when answers to the "why" questions provide vital information, it is "how" that opens the way to change. We cannot change where we have been, but we can change where we are going. The change is in our hands. That is part of recovering from the wounds of the past. Unless we change what we are doing in the present, we will continue to duplicate the past. For many victims of abuse, the path they take in the present must go back to the past. Their future is their past.

I vividly recall a lesson I learned from a young man years ago. He was eighteen years old, with an impressive, handsome face and strong shoulders. I was a chaplain intern in a hospital in Houston, Texas. It was summer 1959. Never had I faced his kind of anger and despair. Day after day he raged and cried. I sat anxiously, listening to his sobs and curses. I listened, not because I realized the value of listening but because I was afraid of him, drawn to him. His anger and questions about himself and life and God so frightened me that I did not know how to respond.

"Why, chaplain? Why did I lose my feet?" He asked the question again and again. "Why did this happen to me? Why? Why did this happen?"

After several weeks I finally reached a point where I could no longer listen to his painful crying and his endless demand that someone tell him why he had lost both of his feet just above the ankles. On that day my anxiety overwhelmed my clinical training.

"Mike, you keep asking why? why?... You want to know why you lost both of your feet—why this happened to you? Mike, it happened because you were hit by a car that pinned you against the bumper of another car. You lost both of your feet because a friend drove to where you were standing behind your car. He was acting like a fool and tried to scare you. He waited too long to put on his brakes. He hit you with his car. That is WHY you lost your feet. Mike, that is the only reason it happened—because of the stupidity of a friend."

My response was as startling to me as it was to Mike. We both were silent for a few moments. I rose to leave.

"Mike, I'm sorry I can't help you with the 'why.' That is the reason why, and there is nothing either of us can do about it. I wish I could make it a terrible dream but I can't. I am going to leave, but I'll be back. When you are ready to face the question of 'how'—how you, a handsome, eighteen-year-old man can go on living a meaningful and happy life without two feet, I'll do all I can to help you figure that out."

He did, and I did—and he did!

It may sound trite. Needed changes in our lives are usually fairly simple but rarely if ever easy. How do people get past the bad things that happen? How do they overcome the traumas that cause wounded, compromised, and maladjusted lives? How do people change?

I referred earlier to Paul's statement, "Do not be conformed to this world, but be transformed by the renewing of your mind" (Rom 12:2). Paul's simple challenge is pregnant with a theology and psychology essential to overcoming the wounds of abuse and tragedy. What Paul says is fundamental to every school of psychology, a major underpinning of the Christian religion and many other world religions as well.

One of the ongoing mental tasks we face daily is that of sorting out our thoughts. What is true? What is real? Which is of greater value? Which is more important: what we think or what others think? When is one more appropriate than the other? These points are critical for abused persons. Therapy addresses the need to change thoughts that are excess baggage from the past into those that more accurately or appropriately reflect the present. This is immeasurably critical to effecting and sustaining behavioral changes. Psychologically, Paul challenges his readers not to conform to the thinking of the Greek world—the age in which they lived—but to change their way of thinking about their lives based on a different rationale for their world. Theologically, Paul cites the context for new thinking as God's grace—the "mercies of God." Paul urges his readers to free themselves from invalid thinking based on concepts void of grace. It is the grace of God—God's good intentions toward us, God's involvement with us in our life—that provides a foundation for the risk and the daring to form new thinking and new living.

The way out of the dark night of the soul is new thinking—new thinking about God, one's self, and the meaning of the scars. Carl Jung recognized this when he wrote:

> Among all of my patients in the second half of life—that is to say, over thirty-five—there has not been one whose problem in the last resort was not that of finding a religious outlook on life....Everyone of them fell ill because he had lost that which the living religions of ev-

ery age have given to their fellows, and none of them has been really healed who did not regain his religious outlook.[2]

When Jung spoke of religion, he was not speaking of a collection of beliefs or an organized group called a church. Jung understood religion as "the attitude peculiar to a consciousness which has been altered by the experience of the *numinosum*."[3] Jung was thinking of the way a person thinks and lives in response to an experience with the living God. Jung uses the term *numinosum* when he speaks of one's experience with God as a dynamic, invisible, life-engendering reality.

Jung was the son of a Swiss Lutheran minister. He spent his childhood and youth "in church." He had a solid exposure to the Bible and to the theological influence of his minister father. But Jung did not believe in God. Two years before his death in 1961, Jung appeared on the BBC television program, "Face to Face." John Freeman, the interviewer, asked him, "Do you believe in God?" Jung replied, "Believe? No—I know!" For Jung, belief had to do with creeds and dogmas about God. God has to do with personal experience and with knowing the phenomenon of grace.

One result of the church's efforts over the past two thousand years to fix the truth about God in the biblical canon is a shift that focuses on believing what others have said about their experience with God. The Bible is filled with the records of what people came to know about God through their experiences. It is not just a collection of beliefs about God. It is, at the core, a record of those experiences people had with God over the centuries. It is also true that much of what the Bible contains is the inspired personal opinions and conclusions of the writers. While these opinions and conclusions are true, we tend to set them up as a guarantee that if we duplicate them we will have the same experience. Jung's affirmation of his personal experience with God reflects the biblical use of the word knowledge— to be intimately acquainted with. In scripture a word for knowledge was often used to describe the sexual relationship between a man and a woman—they *knew* each other.

We cannot separate psychology and theology or psychology and religion. Each, in part, is a description of the same essence—being and meaning in human experience. Jung suggests that every crisis, by its very nature, is spiritual. To me, life by its very nature is a spiritual odyssey. I have not encountered a counselee or a student whose conflicts and stresses in life were not, in the final analysis, tied to their image of God, their image of themselves, and their image of the scars they bear. This is especially true of victims of tragedy and abuse. Thomas's image of God was very much a part of his question: *Where was God when I was raped?"*

Image of God

> *"Karen, I want you to draw a picture of God."*
> *"Huh?"* she gasped. *"Draw a picture of God? Uh-uh, no way; I couldn't do that,"* she blurted, shaking her head. *"No way…."*

A few weeks later Karen handed me her drawing of God. At first glance, I concealed my surprise. Her drawing was on a small square piece of white paper. It consisted of a music staff with numerous types of notes floating about the paper. The different notes were in bright and pastel colors. The atmosphere of the picture was light. Only the lines on the staff were black and heavy. Even this seemed normal. As I studied Karen's picture, I was confused. She had drawn many pictures during the past months, but this one was the first that was not dark, foreboding, and depressing. Karen's explanation was simple: "God is God; he is good and beautiful and everything right."

How did that match the bad image she had of herself? How could she believe in that kind of God? It was all quite logical. Karen pictured God as all good, and music was one of the few good things in life. God's goodness brought her badness into a clearer focus. Thus Karen saw God as something beautiful and good—like music. But God's goodness only accented her badness. To her, God was like a beautiful piece of music that only a really good musician could play. Karen could appreciate and listen to the music (God), but she could never adequately play it. God was remote and always beyond any real, personal interaction.

It was easy to understand why the concept of a God who lived within caused Karen such distress. Hers was a long journey. It was filled with many hours of practice before Karen began to accept the music within her.

The pictures we draw are revealing. A whole system of therapy is built around the use of various art media. I am not a trained art therapist, but I recognize that a person's picture of God is often a powerful statement of his or her concept of God. Even people who disclaim belief in God or claim that God is not important to them are often intrigued with what their picture of God reveals.

Trudy was a religious woman and a faithful church member, but she needed counseling to deal with anxiety. She suffered from agoraphobia (fear of open places) and an occasional bout of tachycardia (rapid heartbeat). She talked candidly about her religious life and her faith in God. She prayed often, went to church regularly, and contributed faithfully to the church. All of this added to her frustration as she grew more fearful. In addition, she was dreaming that she divorced her husband and ran away from her family—two things she would never do.

When Trudy talked of God, I got an image of a nice old man with a bad temper who, at times, carried a big stick. When she drew a picture of God, she drew a young boy. The boy had neither hands nor feet, and was dressed in a white robe. His handless arms were open in a welcoming gesture. When she described her drawing, she said it was a "picture of Jesus." She was not aware it was a child Jesus who had neither hands nor feet.

Trudy was in a psychological and spiritual bind. She could no longer tolerate much that was happening in her life. She was on the verge of a change in her vocation and a possible divorce. The latter was beyond her conscious awareness. These actions were unacceptable to her parents and to her husband.

Trudy's image of God blocked her from the resources of her own faith. Her God was a perfect being who demanded perfection from her. Her God was at times a kind old grandfather, but more often he emerged in her thoughts as a stern old man who judged and punished boys and girls without mercy when they did something wrong. This is the message she retained from her childhood. She dared not talk to her God about her real problems. She could talk to Jesus; he could protect her from the old man's anger. But subconsciously even Jesus was powerless as a child without hands or feet. Her Jesus was kind and gentle with open arms. But he was just a child. How could he know anything about the complexities of adult life? She wanted to live a life that would appease and please God, the old man, but it just didn't work. She remained naive and fearful in the real adult world, much like a confused and helpless adolescent.

There were paradoxes and distortions of reality in her life—

controlling parents, an abusive marriage, legalistic religious training. Her God—the old man God—her family, and her church would not tolerate her thoughts about divorce and changes in lifestyle. Her young Jesus could not understand the sexual frustrations of an adult woman whose husband had for ten years preferred physical exercise to a sexual relation with her.

The last picture of God that Trudy drew for me was the face of a pleasant, bright-looking adult woman. She drew it spontaneously. Trudy's emphasis was on the woman's head. Trudy overcame her agoraphobia, found new ways to reduce her anxieties, and made choices about her life. How did she do this? A critical part of her work focused on Paul's words in the twelfth chapter of Romans. She discovered God's grace in a new way; she began to experience God's grace in herself. The fearful God of her childhood gave way to a God of grace who loved her—who was with her—in her. Surprisingly, when she changed her way of thinking about God, the God of the Bible became more real than ever.

Trudy found confidence and power to face life as an adult with a God who lives in her, loves her, encourages her, strengthens her. God, no longer a superman who lives in the sky, became the living, dynamic, and personal God in the core of her life. God became less the someone she believed in, but more of what Joseph Campbell terms "the personification of that world-creative energy and mystery which is beyond thinking and naming."[4] For me, this names God as more than traditional Christian theology ever has. It is to image God as the totally Other—a divine mystery beyond comprehension, yet more personally and intimately knowable than any other human being.

I am reminded again of Paul's statement at the close of his poetic definition of love. After his eloquent and demanding description of what love is, Paul adds: "When I was a child I spoke like a child, I thought like a child, I reasoned like a child; when I became a man, I gave up childish ways" (1 Cor 13:11). It is hard for an adult to live in the real world of adulthood with childhood images of God. Paul makes it clear that the God of adulthood is not a policeman, an old man with a stick, an angry demanding judge, or an ideal parent. The God who is, is more than any concept of human personhood can contain. We can describe and define God in terms of our human reality, but we forget that God is not limited to our reality. To the same degree that we reject the mystery of God, we are doomed to make God predictably human.

One of the most powerful forces that has contributed to my image of God has been the Western culture and mindset, a reality I was unaware of for many years. The American religious community is in general ignorant of how much our thoughts about God and our images of God have filtered through several hundred years of Western culture. Consequently, when we read the Bible, we read it with minds geared to think in Western rational, literal, and concrete terms. This is not totally bad, but it does force the Bible into a cultural and conceptual framework which is foreign to the people and time that produced it. Living and working among the people of Saudi Arabia during the Persian Gulf War made me acutely aware how Western and Eastern rationale are different—not good or bad—but different. Jesus, for example, thought with an Eastern mind; he was a person of symbols and mystery. Jesus understood and related from the Eastern experience of what is. Jesus' image of God was more than his definitions or his symbols. Jesus' definition of God was who and what God was doing in and through him at any given moment. That was the God he knew, but even that was not all there is to God. Joseph Campbell calls attention to the danger that lies in a religious awareness highly contaminated by the Western mind.

What the Eastern teachers are telling us is that...the Divine lives within you. Our Western religions tend to put the Divine outside of the earthly world in God, in heaven. But the whole sense of the Oriental is that the kingdom of heaven is within you. Who is in heaven? God is. Where's God? God's within you. It is this kind of Eastern mind-set out of which Jesus said, "The kingdom of God is within you."

We think not only that our God has been named and known but that He's given us a whole system of rules. But the system of rules...are [only] man's clues as to how to get the realization of God. Their [Eastern] view is quite different from that. When you hear it, you say, "Ah, yes."[5]

Some commonly held images of God include the Ruler of the Universe, the Bookkeeper of deeds, the perfect Father, the eternal Policeman, the Divine Administrator of resources, the Divine Dispenser of human requests, and so on. I am convinced that a key to overcoming the bad in life—and maximizing the use of good—is an image of God that centers in the energizing dynamic of grace.

One of the best known parables of Jesus is the "Parable of the

Prodigal Son" (Lk 15:11-32). This is really a misnomer since the story actually deals with the prodigal behavior of both sons. The parable develops two powerful themes: the psycho-spiritual opposites of the two sons and the foundational theme of the father's incomprehensible grace. In the story, every action and non-action ascribed to the father is symbolic of what God's grace is like in human experience. Jesus says this is who God is and how God relates to us. It is interesting to discover how uncomfortable each of the sons is with the father's grace.

"A certain man had two sons; and he divided his wealth between them. The younger gathered everything together and went on a journey. He squandered his estate with loose living. When he had spent everything, a famine occurred. He went and attached himself to one of the citizens. And he sent him into his fields to feed swine. And he was longing to fill his stomach with the pods that the swine were eating. And when he came to his senses, he said, 'I will go to my father and will say to him, 'Father, I have sinned against heaven and in your sight. I am no longer worthy to be called your son; make me as one of your hired men.'

"...and he came to his father...[and] said to him, 'Father, I have sinned against heaven and in your sight. I am no longer worthy to be called your son.'

"But the father said, 'Quickly bring out the best robe and put it on him and put a ring on his hand and sandals on his feet; and bring the fatted calf, kill it, and let us eat and be merry.'

"Now the older son was in the field and when he came...he heard music and dancing.... He became angry and was not willing to go in, and his father came out and began entreating him. But he answered and said to his father, 'Look! For so many years I have been serving you and I have never neglected a command of yours; and yet you have never given me a kid that I might be merry with my friends. But when this son of yours came who has devoured your wealth with harlots, you killed the fattened calf for him.'

"And he said to him, 'My child, you have always been with me and all that is mine is yours. But we had to be merry and rejoice for this brother of yours was dead and has begun to live....' "6

As is often true of great storytellers, Jesus did not give a conclusion to this story. Instead, he left a great deal to the imagination and experience of his hearers to fill in and expand upon. I have my own version of the scene that likely occurred after the welcome-home party was over. It goes like this.

The guests make their way home. The older son is in the kitchen checking that the dishes are in their proper place and all the silverware is accounted for. The father and the younger son are alone in the banquet hall. The father takes a sip of wine, smiles, and says, "Son, it is good to have you home."

"Thanks, Dad, it is good. But there's something I have to get straight. I don't understand all of this. When I came home today, I told you I didn't deserve to be a son any longer." Looking around the room he continues, "I don't deserve all of this. I don't deserve to be treated like this. I tried earlier to tell you how bad I've been."

"I know," the father replies, his smile fading a bit. "I know, but I told you I forgive you."

"That's the part I don't understand. Dad, I don't deserve your forgiveness. I wasted every penny you gave me on every foolish and sinful kind of activity you can imagine."

"I know and I forgive you," the father persists.

"But, Dad, there's got to be something more to this. I mean…"

"Well, Son," the smile is gone and the father's eyes fill with tears, "there is something more to it."

"I knew it. I knew there was more to it. What's the catch?"

"Son, there is no catch. I do forgive you for all the bad and dumb stuff you've done. What you did was foolish and it was wrong. But more important, Son, I forgive you for why you did it. I forgive you for the reason you did those things."

The father leaves the son pondering his words. *"He forgives me for what I did? I told him I didn't deserve to be his son because of all the evil things I've done and he says, 'I forgive you—I forgive you for the REASON you did what you did.' The REASON I did what I did?"*

The father enters the kitchen and the older brother looks up from his ledger. "Dad, I'm glad it's you. I was hoping you'd come out here so I could talk to you."

"What's wrong, Son? something missing?"

"No, Dad, nothing like that. I just need to get something straight about our conversation this afternoon."

"What don't you understand?" the father asks.

"Well, Dad, I can't understand this thing about your forgiving me.

I told you this afternoon I had not disobeyed any of your instructions. I reminded you that I'd kept the company policies and had run things strictly by your book."

"Yes, I know, Son, and I assured you that I forgave you for it."

"But that's just the point, Dad. I didn't do anything wrong. Not once did I come in late or quit early. I've worked hard and didn't waste time or money on a party in all these years. And you forgive me? You forgive him for being bad and forgive me for being good. That doesn't make any sense to me."

"Well, Son," the father replies in a gentle voice, "it is not that I forgive you for being good and obeying the rules. There is nothing wrong with doing good. In fact, it's the right thing to do—to keep the rules. But, Son, I forgive you for *why* you did it. I forgive you for the reason you've been good all these years."

God's intentions toward us are good. The father was with both sons, loved both sons, understood both sons, and was gracious to both of them. The father's gratuitousness did not depend on whether they were good or bad. Rather, the ground for his grace was his own nature. It was his nature and unalterable choice to be gracious to them. What Jesus is saying is that we are powerless to divert God's grace regardless of what we do. This grace invites us to relationship with the power and meaning of the divine. God does not want our disobedience; that can be harmful to our well-being. The younger son proves this. Neither does God want our obedience. That, too, can be harmful to our well-being. The older son proves this. God wants us to be aware that it is not what we do or do not do that brings us into relationship. It is our relationship to God, to grace. We can accept this relationship of grace and live in it, or ignore it, reject it, and go on existing without its meaning and power. We do this by rebelling against the rules or compulsively obeying them. The result is the same. We miss the meaning and power of personal relationship with God.

An old story illustrates this. A Buddhist monk saw a scorpion entangled in the massive web-like roots of a tree. A swollen river surrounded the tree and the scorpion was about to be swept away by the rushing current of the flooded river. The monk reaches his hand out again and again to rescue the scorpion. Each time the creature stings his would-be friend. The monk continues his rebuffed efforts. A student of the monk watching the apparent senseless drama remarks,

"Your hands are swollen and bleeding from his stings. Why do you keep trying to rescue the scorpion when he keeps stinging you for your efforts?" The monk replies, "The scorpion stings because it is his nature. I continue to try to rescue him because it is my nature. Shall the scorpion's nature to sting keep me from my nature to love?"

Image of self

Karen struggled with drawing a picture of God. She had less difficulty drawing pictures of herself. Her early ones were nondescript lines and scribbles that developed into nonhuman forms. They looked something like a cross between a robot and a cartoon concept of the devil with a red tail shaped like a pitchfork. Others were dark, lifeless forms—tubes, boxes, and bars—accented with red for anger, blue for pain, and sparse traces of green for life. Her drawings were filled with chains, ropes, walls, and chests with closed locks. In her own words, Karen was "bad, evil, worthless, and a biological mistake." She remembered overhearing her mother say on several occasions, "I should have had an abortion. I wish you had never been born."

Psychologists and sociologists tell us of the power that the self-image has in determining what we think and feel and how we behave. Our earliest experiences have an impact on our development toward a sense of who we are. There is no greater negative impact to one's self-image than sexual abuse. This is especially true when those within a family perpetrate abuse. As Peck notes, children assimilate responsibility for the evil someone does to them. And with many, like Karen, the assimilation is so comprehensive that the evil becomes the substance of the image they have of themselves. It is imperative that people change their image of self before they can free themselves from the "bad stuff" that happens to them. Serenity addressed this reality in her reflections on my manuscript:

> If I let go of the rage, the pain, the fear, will there be anything left of me? The effects of the abuse are what I have always known myself to be: angry, wounded, and frightened. This is not a description of what I am like, but who I believe I am: "I am anger; I am wound; I am fear." So what *will* I be? Will I even exist if I let go of them? To let go of this is to let go of me. Can I believe that I am more than that?

How hard it is to believe that there is more to my being...what grace to move from believing myself to be the effects of my abuse—angry, wounded, and frightened—to believing that the abuse affected me. It is hard to move from believing that I am what happened to me to believing that evil was done to me, that the evil abused my sanctity, that the God within me was desecrated and violated.... If I am what happened to me, then there is no hope for healing.[7]

The images we form of ourselves develop slowly. They also die slowly. This is especially true when they are negative images associated with wrongs that children experience. Karen's drawings as well as Sarah's charted a slow but consistent change in her self-image. I remember the day she brought in the drawing of a little girl of about ten or twelve. She wore a long dress with an apron, and an old-fashioned bonnet covered her head. The child was lively, striding though a disarray of frame-like objects that symbolized pain. There was so much life and positive movement apparent in the child that I lost my composure. Karen noticed my brightened effect.

"Karen, as you can tell, I like that little girl. She is alive. She has guts. She is going to make it through all that pain and stuff!" I waited, the hint of a smile on her face.

Karen's drawing brought forth a new spark of hope! A second drawing duplicated the same scene and Karen added a second figure—a young boy. The children, determined in their journey, were moving in a common direction through the pain. Their projected paths would merge. The picture was, nevertheless, still filled with ominous symbols of pain and anger.

"She still has a long way to go," Karen said. "You can see a lot of anger and pain there." She pointed to the black border and the red doorway that the young boy had entered.

"But see that?" Karen pointed to the yellowish haze around the boy. "That is hope. He has already come through a lot of stuff, and he will help her. Anyway, she's not alone anymore...."

Changing bad images is painful. It takes tremendous self-talk, experience with grace, and hard work. Some years ago there was much emphasis in the literature of popular psychology about "self-talk," "scripting," and "internal tapes." People were urged to re-program the verbal messages they carried from childhood. That approach is valid. We do have to confront the messages in the script. Many of those messages come from parental figures, some from our own concepts. These images and messages cannot be taken lightly since they are powerful and affect our lives daily. They are our reality, more real than anything else.

When one deals with self-images, what is real to a person is more powerful than what is true. Margery Williams illustrates this in *The Velveteen Rabbit*. The Skin Horse is talking about something positive—being loved and becoming a real person. But his succinct definition of personal reality applies doubly to the negative aspects of life and being unloved.

> "What is REAL?" asked the Rabbit one day...
> "Real isn't how you are made," the Skin Horse said. "It's a thing that happens to you."[8]

Most real to us is what we believe about what happens to us.

I often assign self-affirming messages for people to read. On such occasions I write the assignments much like a prescription to be taken three or four times daily. Many people make light of this strategy. I often hear, "That's silly. I can't go around telling myself good things. That doesn't help." Yet those same people will repeat a litany of negative things about themselves every day of their lives. Such negative self-talk is so natural and ingrained that they are often not aware how it dominates their conversations.

Changing one's self-image is difficult, but it is an imperative in the healing process. The Apostle Paul wrote about self-image in his statement about the need to change one's thinking. He says, "For by the grace of God...I bid every one among you not to think of himself more highly than he ought to think, but to think with sober judgment..." (Rm 12:3). What Paul says in a negative manner is that the image we have of ourselves should be accurate. People should not have inflated self-images, but they should not allow themselves to have deflated self-images either. One's self-image should be built with sound judgment grounded in the reality of God's grace. God's grace invites the change, but grace is not pushy. The choice for change is always an individual one, and the challenge is the use of sound judgment.

Ironweed is about grace and the inability to change one's self-image. In the movie, Jack Nicholson plays Francis Phelan, a bum on the streets of Albany, New York, in the late 1930s. Two tragic events mar Francis's life. As a young boy he is caught up in a mob of angry

Teamsters on strike. Carried away by the emotion of the crowd, Francis throws a rock, mortally wounding a scab trolley car driver. The memory of killing the young man will not leave Francis. Then, as a young father, Francis accidentally drops his infant son and the child dies of a broken neck.

Francis cannot live with his evil deeds. Unable to accept the forgiveness of others, unable to forgive himself, Francis leaves his family and takes to the streets and to the bottle. He lives out his unforgiving self. He is a man so marred, so wrong, that he is beyond hope of change; Francis sees himself beyond forgiveness. Like many victims of abuse, Francis assimilates the wrongs he did unintentionally and equates the essence of who he is with what he has done. He is committed to living out the past in the present and perpetuates the responsibility for the past. In so doing, he rejects responsibility for the present without which there can be no hope for the future. Francis's present becomes an endless journey into the past.

Francis frequents the street missions. He listens with a deaf ear to the sermons of grace and forgiveness. He ignores the hope of starting over in life. He is there for soup, not sermon; survival, not living. During a brief return visit, his wife offers him his old home. He refuses and tells his now grown daughter he is beyond forgiveness. He refuses to consider what a sober family life in the present might mean.

As the movie ends, Francis rides along in an empty boxcar, clutching his bottle of whiskey. He sees a vision. His wife (a Mrs. Job character) is sitting on a crate pouring tea. She asks, "What do you need, Francis?" He needs grace, forgiveness, and hope.

He replies, "A turkey sandwich would be nice."

Francis could never change what happened nor could he ever fully atone for it—not in a thousand lifetimes of wine bottles. He spends his life trying to change the past. Refusing to be responsible for living in the present, he had no future.[9]

For many victims of abuse, where they are going in the present is back to the past. Their future is their past.

Karen could not change her past. Unlike Francis Phelan, she was not responsible for the wrong in her past. Karen was the victim of the evil actions and mistakes of others. She had lived most of her life bound to it as if it were her fault. She, too, imagined herself beyond forgiveness, beyond change and hope for a life free from anger and guilt, pain and despair. This did not begin to change until she claimed responsibility for the present and used sound judgment in facing her responsibility for the present.

In chapter five I stated that we are the focus of God's grace whether we like it or not. We are powerless before God's intention to be gracious to us just as God is powerless to control our lives and make us gracious to each other. We are powerless to control God's grace. Nevertheless, in the midst of such powerlessness, there resides the greatest power in the universe: the power of grace! The grace of God influences the grace of men and women: the unmerited, undeserved good intentions of one toward another. This is not only a new ethic for human relationships, it is a new ethic and a new power for changing our individual images. Again, it is not new in the sense that it has never been, but it is new in the sense of awareness, becoming ever new as one becomes aware. Like the purple flowers in an open field, "it" has been ignored too long in the fields of personal identity—in our relationship with ourselves.

Here is a different motivation for the Karens and the Thomases, the Sarahs and the Horaces to treat themselves graciously. Here is the true justification for looking at one's self in the mirror and saying, "You are OK!" We need a new image of God as forgiving our best and our worst, a new image of a God who is gracious to us, a new image of ourselves as graced and forgiven, invited—urged—to leave the empty boxcars of life that are ever-traveling and never getting anywhere. The Francises and the Karens must dare to start over again and again and again. We weave the fabric of meaning with which we clothe our lives out of what we believe about what happens to us.

Karen had to look in the mirror to face the responsibility of what she saw—God in her—gracing her with an opportunity to start living each day anew.

Image of the scars

Interwoven with the images of God and of self are the scars, scars not so much of the body as of the soul. People do not live through experiences with evil and tragedy without being scarred. This book is not about the therapeutic how-to's of change. It is a book about how change can occur, about the power and energy for activating change.

However, there is a need to make observations about this vital issue. How do people deal effectively with the scars of life?

I envision a collage of faces, the faces of men and women who have taught me much of what I know about God and grace, evil and scars, healing and change. I see the faces of Karen, Sarah, Elizabeth, Beth, Thomas, Laura, Tom, Barbara, and dozens of others. They have allowed me to see their scars, to examine the hardened, calloused spots, to touch the tender, unhealed areas. My eyes have welled with tears in those sacred moments when a person exposes his or her scars and in that moment becomes vulnerable once again. The context in that moment must be grace and the guiding principle, sound judgment. Some therapists call it therapeutic integrity; Carl Rogers calls it unconditional positive regard. As a rose by any other name is still a rose, so grace by any other term is still grace.

The numerous scars of abuse and tragedy take on an endless array of designs. I am aware of a few of the crucial scars. Let me name a few.

- The scars of abandonment
- The scars of physical abuse
- The scars of murder
- The scars of mental/emotional abuse
- The scars of senseless tragedy
- The scars of sexual abuse

This list is not complete. At least one other scar is a fundamental result of any experience with evil or random tragedy. It is not only the primary scar, but it is an inseparable part of every abusive experience. In my work I find it the most difficult to deal with and is often the one many overlook. It is the scar of betrayal.

Betrayal leaves a scar that has at least three dimensions. The person who commits the wrong perpetrates the betrayal. This sense of betrayal is present even when the offender is a stranger. This is the basic betrayal of humanity. At times, this may be the least damaging of betrayals, but it is a factor nonetheless. The betrayed is scarred in his or her basic trust of humanity. This experience erodes the underlying need for and the capacity to trust the human community. Obviously, the closer the relationship, the graver the injury, the deeper the scar. In sexual offenses that fathers commit against their daughters, there is an incestuous betrayal of relationship. "How could he do that to me, his own daughter?" is a question that can haunt a woman all of her life.

In cases of incest, the victim seems to feel the deepest betrayal toward the non-abusing parent. Many women have asked, "Why did she let him do it? Why didn't she do something?" There is often an unspoken sense and fear—grounded in fact or not—that the non-participating parent knew what was happening and did nothing about it. Karen and Louise bore the scars of literal betrayal by both parents. Karen, as did Louise, lived with the memory that her mother took part in the sexual abuse of her child.

I recall the dream that a client, J.T., had when she was dealing with her sense of her mother's betrayal. In her dream, J.T. was eating a bowl of soup at the kitchen table. She spied a spider in her soup and begged her mother not to make her eat it. Her mother insisted there was no spider, that J.T. was only making up a lie to avoid eating the soup. She forced the child to eat the soup—and the spider. The implication was too clear to avoid.

Closely related to this sense of betrayal by parents or other adults who should protect them is the betrayal Thomas voiced when he asked, "Where was God when I was being raped as a little boy?" Thomas grew up thinking God and his father betrayed him. It left a deep scar since, like other children, he heard that God is loving and good. God let bad things happen to children only when they were bad, and even then it was for some good reason. This kind of thinking was like a curse to Thomas. Yes, God and his father had betrayed him.

The most insidious and unconscious scar of betrayal is the self-imposed one. It is a complex matter but it must be resolved in the healing process. Betraying one's self is cancerous, and victims do this to themselves mainly to protect their image of someone else: God, mother, father, men, women.

Members of her own family had forced Karen to take part in sexual activities. Conditioned from a young age, she accepted sexual activity as part of family life. It was primary to her survival. On some occasions, she even used her experiences to get what she wanted. Some of these memories made it difficult for her to accept the fact that it still was not her fault, that she was a victim of the power others had over her. Part of what she felt was an unconscious sense of self-betrayal. This issue surfaced again and again.

"I should have killed myself instead of giving in. You say it was their fault. How can it be their fault when I let them keep doing it?"

"Karen, how old were you when your first abuse occurred?" I asked in a matter-of-fact voice.

"Three."

"How old were you when it stopped?"

"Twelve. I know what you are going to say next. 'Who stopped it?' I did. How did it stop? I kept telling people 'til someone finally believed me and did something to help."

Karen believed in her own betrayal so long that she resisted the fact that she had rescued herself. Each person must face responsibility for the betrayal we inflict upon ourselves when we claim the wrongs of our past that really belong to someone else. This is the betrayal we harbor in our souls when we refuse to let go of the images of God, ourselves, and the scars that are distorted, inaccurate, and untrue. This is the ultimate treachery. We betray self when we hold on to the wrongs of yesterday at the expense of today. This was one of Karen's final hurdles—one of her hardest.

How? How do Thomas and Karen, you and I deal with the scars of our wounds? The "how" centers on accepting grace and learning sound judgment. These are two of the three dimensions of true miracles. The third is hard work. Remember Job and J.B.? How did they get back to living life? How did they restore meaning, relationships, and productive activity? In fairy tales, everything is beautiful forever. In real life, miracles don't happen when someone waves a magic wand. They happen by God's grace lived out in faith, sound thinking, and hard work.

What about some of the how-to's? Begin with a commitment to yourself to change—a decision to look at your scars and shout, *"Too long! I have suffered over you too long! I renounce the responsibility for what happened to me. I repent of my wrong and ungracious attitude toward myself. Today I take responsibility to change."* Action needs to follow this commitment.

Read good books. In addition to works mentioned earlier, consider the titles listed at the end of this chapter.[10]

For individual or group help, check local counselors affiliated with the American Association of Pastoral Counselors, the Association for Clinical Pastoral Education, the American Association of Marriage and Family Counselors, the County Mental Health Association, M.S.W. Clinical Social Workers, psychologists, psychiatrists, church and community-sponsored groups such as Alcoholics Anonymous, Alanon, Adult Children of Alcoholics, Abusers Anonymous, or Sexaholics Anonymous.

As I reflect on my experience with the victims of evil and serious tragedy, I have identified several mileposts in the journey of healing—a journey, because healing is not a destination. Rather, it is part of the pilgrimage itself.

Most literature that deals with recovery from significant abuse and tragedy seems to agree with four main phases in the healing process. These stages are the following.

The decision. This is often a long and stressful period, a time when people have to recognize and face the effects of the wrongs they have suffered. Many people live with their secret trauma for twenty to thirty years before they come to a decision to deal with it. In some cases, a delayed reaction or upheaval in life opens the festered wounds to treatment. This demands an acceptance of present responsibility, a choice for change and commitment to action.

The re-engaging. This is a traumatic period. It can rarely be accomplished without professional help and/or support. One begins to deal with memories and suppressed—even repressed—feelings that throw a life into confusion and disorder. It is the tumult of remembering, of facing the reality that it happened, of breaking open the conspiracy of silence, and telling it at last. It is a period of intentional "going home" to the past.

The restructuring. Restructuring one's internal world is slow and demanding work. Its reward is freedom and life. It calls for reevaluating childhood experiences, getting in touch with the child within and validating his/her experience, redistributing fault and guilt, trusting new insights, grieving and mourning real and symbolic losses, facing and accepting anger and finding healthy expressions for it, and finally restructuring the experience in light of adult understanding, compassion, and forgiveness—grace.

The integration. The goal is not to get somewhere. The goal is to get where one chooses to go. As people move through the past and the present, the gradual process of psychological and spiritual integration is occurring.

Two things are important to remember in recovering from significant wounds of the soul. The first step or stage is just that—a stage—nothing more. It is not meant to last forever and will not if you claim the grace and do the work. It will pass.

Second, do not expect to get over whatever happened to you. People do not get over evil and senseless tragedies. How can a child get over being raped? How can a person get over seeing innocent children hanged to death because of their parents' genealogy? We simply do not get over such things. Again, Job, J.B., and Sarah are testimonies to the miracle. The human spirit can recover and adjust; it can live free of, above and beyond evil and wrong. During this period, things begin to come together, to make sense. Old patterns of thinking and behaving give way to revised and new ways. Integration does not mean getting over or rid of something. It does mean that all parts are seen in a different light and treated with new regard individually and collectively. It puts things together in a way that nothing of value is totally lost, and yet we gain something different and new.

Lawrence of Arabia was one of the most colorful figures of the twentieth century. So many stories of his heroics and his adventures make it impossible to separate fact from fable. One of my favorite stories is about a match. One evening Lawrence and some of his companions were relaxing around a fire. Lawrence became preoccupied with striking and extinguishing a match. One of the men seated nearby watched him intently.

Lawrence would strike a match, hold it up, and stare at the flame. After a moment he would extinguish the flame between his thumb and finger. Each time he snuffed out the flame, he'd strike another match and repeat the ritual. A companion watching him became curious and finally tried the same feat. He struck a match, stared at it for a moment, then moved to put it out with thumb and finger. As the flesh of his fingers touched the flame of the match, the man pulled his hand back. Again he advanced thumb and finger to put out the flame. Again, he withdrew as finger and flame met. After several attempts he turned to Lawrence and said, "That hurts; what's the trick?"

"The trick?" Lawrence replied. "The trick is in not caring that it hurts."

The challenge of the present is to be bigger than the hurts of the past.

If you get where you are going,
Where will you be?
Today you have a choice...
Make it.

You are more than
what happens to you—
You can be bigger
than the hurt.

NOTES

1. *Alice's Adventures in Wonderland* in *Complete Works of Lewis Carroll* (New York: Random House, Inc., 1947), pp. 71-72.

2. C.J. Jung, *Modern Man in Search of a Soul* (New York: Harcourt, Brace, 1922), p. 229.

3. C.J. Jung, *Psychology and Religion* (New Haven, Connecticut: Yale University Press, 1950), pp. 5-7.

4. John Maher and Dennie Briggs, eds., *An Open Life: Joseph Campbell in Conversation with Michael Toms* (New York: Larson Publications, 1988), p. 64.

5. Ibid., p. 64

6. Some interpreters note that the father was not *with* the prodigal son until he came home. It seems, however, that the son's experience was different. In verses 18 and 21 the son claims that his sin was done "before" the father, in sight of the father. Psychologically and theologically speaking, the younger son experienced his father as very much with him all those years.

7. "Do Not Let Your Servant Vanish," reflections on *Where Is God When Bad Things Happen?* by "Serenity" (the name given her by another victim of abuse). I remain thankful for Serenity's gift.

8. Margery Williams, *The Velveteen Rabbit* (Philadelphia: Running Press, 1989), pp. 18, 20.

9. William Kennedy, *Ironweed* (New York: Penguin Books, 1984).

10. M. Scott Peck, *The Road Less Traveled* (New York: Touchstone Books, 1980) and Alice and Walden Howard, *Exploring the Road Less Traveled* (New York: Touchstone Books, 1985), a workbook to accompany Peck's book; John Powell, *Why Am I Afraid to Tell You Who I Am?* (Allen

Texas: Tabor Publishing, rev. ed., 1990); John Sanford, *The Kingdom Within* (New York: Harper & Row, Inc., rev. ed., 1987); Wendy Maltz and Beverly Holman, *Incest and Sexuality* (Lexington, Massachusetts: Lexington Books, 1986); Eliana Gil, *Outgrowing the Pain* (New York: Dell, 1988); Margo Adair, *Working Inside Out* (Berkeley, California: Wingbow Press, 1985); Harriet Goldhor Lerner, *The Dance of Anger* (New York: Harper & Row, Inc., 1989); and informational self-help books such as Pamela Vredevelt and Kathryn Rodriguez, *Surviving the Secret* (Old Tappan, New Jersey: Fleming H. Revell, Inc., 1987) and Ellen Bass and Laura Davis, *The Courage to Heal* (New York: Harper & Row, Inc., 1988), Charles L. Allen, *God's Psychiatry* (Old Tappan, New Jersey: Fleming H. Revell, Inc., 1984).

Epilogue

"I'll start, Chaplain," Thomas blurted.

He was twenty-four years old. There was still a boyish cast to his face, but something in his eyes denied innocence. His eyes spoke of dark alleys and long nights.

"Where was God when I was raped?" Thomas's question was blunt and unexpected.

That was more than three years ago, but his words are as fresh in my mind today as they were during that spiritual values session. What happened to me that day marked the beginning of a new journey into my own faith and understanding of God. The pages you have read document more than anything else what that journey has been like for me. If it has been valuable to you, I am pleased. If it has not, I am sorry. But that, too, is OK. It continues to be of value to me.

What has become of Thomas and Karen? How do their stories end? They don't end; the last page is not yet written.

Thomas was discharged the day after our spiritual values group. He returned to his job as a professional in the field of human services and to his therapy. Our paths have not crossed again. I think of him often and am grateful for our brief but, for me, life-enriching encounter.

At this writing, Karen is still in therapy. Our sessions continue to challenge our respective understanding of ourselves and our awareness of God's presence within us. She continues her journey into maturity and independence. She will complete her college work and looks forward to a career as a helping professional in social service or counseling.

Thomas, Sarah, Karen, and the others have taught me much about God and the incredible wonder and power of grace. For this I shall be forever grateful. They are indeed theologians-in-residence-of-everyday-life.

Let me introduce you to one more person. People like her continue to teach me what life can be like when we live by the grace of a God who is within us every minute of every day.

I do not know her name; yet her name is legion. Her sisters and brothers fill the cities and hamlets of our world. In their honor, I call her Carla. Carla appeared to be in her late forties, a resident in a women's downtown hotel. She came to visit a friend who was a patient in our hospital. She and a chaplain were the only persons in the elevator. She was a thin woman. She was wearing dark polyester pants, a dark blouse, and a large off-white coat sweater. Her hair was slightly unkempt. She leaned against the side of the elevator near the elevator buttons. The chaplain said, "Hi, could you punch 'three' for me. Thanks."

"It's been a hard day," Carla said, her lips beginning to quiver. "I'm going to visit a friend who is sick and I just came from the funeral of my closest friend."

The elevator opened on the third floor. The chaplain hesitated. She looked at Carla and asked, "Would you mind if I rode to five with you? There's a nice lounge right off the elevator. Maybe we could take a few minutes before your visit to talk about this hard day."

Carla quickly responded. "I'd like that." As they sat down, Carla said, "Mary was my closest friend. My life was in pieces, like a puzzle I couldn't put together. But Mary believed in me. She changed my life; she loved me." Tears and sniffles interrupted Carla's story. "Today at her funeral her family didn't speak to me. They probably thought, 'There's that street person Carla over there…. She's nothing.' And you know what Mary would have said? She'd have smiled and said, 'Carla, rise above it—I love you.' I know it shouldn't get me down, but it does now and then—I mean what folks think about me. I mean, I'm just human, and it does hurt when people look at ya like you are nothing. I shouldn't be crying like this, but…but it hurts."

The chaplain replied, "Yeah."

Carla continued. "I've known a lot of hurts. I had it rough growing up. My parents were alcoholics. I was abused and unloved at home. I've been raped…and beat up." Carla's cheeks were wet with tears. Her voice broke as she continued. "I remember once I wrote my mama a letter and told her how much I loved her. D'ya know what she said? She said, 'Don't ya have nothin' better ta do with your time?' She never said she loved me. She couldn't. So, at sixteen, I ran away from home for good. I know what it is like to live on the streets. I did it for a while. But I know God is with me. You know the hotel where I live? They let women who just got out of prison come there too. Some are scared of 'em. But I embrace them. I'm not afraid of the prostitutes, alcoholics, addicts. You know John 3:16: 'For God so loved the world…' is powerful for me. But Luke 15 about the prodigal son is too. I see every one of those people on the streets wearing that cloak of the prodigal son. They are wounded and I know God loves them and I love them. They are human beings. They make mistakes…. You know them homes for unwed mothers? I know the pain and darkness they go through trying to decide whether to keep their babies or if it's best to give 'em up. I know 'cuz I was in that kind o' home myself."

The chaplain sat silently, holding Carla's hands as she cried.

"You know," Carla continued as she gained her composure, "I believe God loves that man who killed all them children down there in California.[1] He had a deep wound. If only somebody could have got to him and seen it. You know you gotta love with your heart, not with your eyes. Your eyes see hard things. The love has gotta come from your heart. Do you agree?"

"Yes, I agree," the chaplain said. "The distance from the eyes to the heart is sometimes a long way."

"Ya know," Carla began again, "I believe God is calling me to be a minister. It may sound funny, but a minister right on the streets…. But who am I to be tellin' you this? Here you are, a real minister. I often wonder if ministers have problems. Do they get together and talk?"

"Sometimes, lots of times," the chaplain replied. "So here we are, a couple of ministers, talking about problems and pain…and God."

Carla smiled. "Ya know another thing I think is important? Humility. We are all human beings. There is a Catholic priest in town that just died of AIDS."

"Yes, I know. You mean Peter Davis."[2]

"Yeah, Peter. He had humility. I mean, he got up and told his whole congregation what he done. And you know what? They raised up and stood with him. You know, Peter walked all the ways across a room once just to shake my hand. I went to his funeral. I ain't no Catholic, but he sure made me feel special."

"Ya know Michael Stoops[3] was another one. He was judged too hard. He's a human being. I went to Baloney Joe's mission for Thanksgiving one year. You should have seen them little street kids crawling out of cold cars or from under the bridge, so tickled to have a hot meal. He done a lotta good for the street people all over. He was judged too hard."

Carla hesitated. "Sometimes I see the men who raped me. They are human beings, too. They make mistakes—and so do I. Sometimes I think maybe they are sorry. I know I couldn't look at 'em without God's help—and forget it and move on."

Carla and the chaplain parted. Carla went to visit her friend. As the chaplain walked down the hall, she was filled with a strange mixture of feelings and thoughts.

"...When did we see you hungry and feed you, or thirsty and give you drink?...a stranger and welcome you, or naked and clothe you? ...sick or in prison and visit you?"

"As you did it to one of the least of these...you did it to me" (Mt 25:37-40).

* * *

I Was There To Hear Your Borning Cry

I was there to hear your borning cry,
    I'll be there when you are old.
I rejoiced the day you were conceived
    to see your life unfold.
I was there when you were but a child,
    with a faith to suit you well.
In a blaze of light you wandered off
    to find where daemons dwell.
When you heard the wonder of the Word
    I was there to cheer you on.
You were raised to praise the living Lord
    to whom you now belong.

When you find someone to share your time,
and you join your lives as one,
I'll be there to make your verses rhyme
from dusk 'till rising sun.
In the middle ages of your life,
not too old, no longer young,
I'll be there to guide you through the night,
complete what I've begun.
When the evening gently closes in
and you close your weary eyes,
I'll be there as I have always been,
with just one more surprise—
I was there to hear your borning cry,
I'll be there when you are old.
I rejoiced the day you were conceived
to see your life unfold....

* * *

"...*God WITH me*..."

...*a little boy*...

GOD IN ME...."

NOTES

1. Carla spoke of Patrick Edward Purdy, 24. On Tuesday, January 17, 1989, he killed five grade-school children and wounded twenty-nine other children and one school teacher in Stockton, California. The dead children were all refugees from Southeast Asia. Purdy, a felon, used an AK-47 assault rifle purchased from a gun and jewelry shop in Sandy, Oregon. The reason for the massacre remains unknown. After the shooting Purdy killed himself on the school playground.

2. Father Peter Davis, a Jesuit priest and senior pastor of St. Ignatius Parish, Portland, Oregon, was the first priest actively serving a Catholic parish to be diagnosed with acquired immune deficiency syndrome. Fr. Davis

experienced the support of his parish and religious community until his death in December, 1988.

3. Michael Stoops, nationally known advocate for street people; twice awarded Hunthausen Award for Peace Ministry of Oregon. He along with actor Martin Sheen slept on the streets of Washington, D.C. in the winter of 1987 to dramatize the plight of the nation's homeless. He was asked to take a leave of absence and later was removed as director of Baloney Joe's street mission, Portland, Oregon, for allegations of sexual misconduct with street boys who were minors. *Willamette Week,* November 18, 1987.